Remodeling the Universities

Meeting Challenges of the 21st Century

Srinivas K. Saidapur
Former Vice Chancellor
Karnatak University, Dharwad

ATLANTIC
PUBLISHERS & DISTRIBUTORS (P) LTD

Published by
ATLANTIC
PUBLISHERS & DISTRIBUTORS (P) LTD
7/22, Ansari Road, Darya Ganj, New Delhi-110002
Phones : +91-11-40775252, 40775214, 23273880, 23275880
Fax: +91-11-23285873
Web: www.atlanticbooks.com
E-mail: orders@atlanticbooks.com

Disclaimer

- The author and the publisher have taken every effort to the maximum of their skill, expertise and knowledge to provide correct material in the book. Even then if some mistakes persist in the content of the book, the publisher does not take responsibility for the same. The publisher shall have no liability to any person or entity with respect to any loss or damage caused, or alleged to have been caused directly or indirectly, by the information contained in this book.
- The author has fully tried to follow the copyright law. However, if any work is found to be similar, it is unintentional and the same should not be used as defamatory or to file legal suit against the author.
- If the readers find any mistakes, we shall be grateful to them for pointing out those to us so that these can be corrected in the next edition.
- All disputes are subject to the jurisdiction of Delhi courts only.

Printed & bound in India by Atlantic Print Services

Dedication

In fond memory, this book is dedicated to late Prof. M.I. Savadatti, former Vice Chancellor, Mangalore University; member, the University Grants Commission, New Delhi; a distinguished educationist; and a scientist who toiled lifelong for promotion and spread of higher education and popularization of science, particularly in North Karnataka

Opinions on the Book

'Remodeling the Universities', this timely contribution by an eminent and hands-on academic, addresses the long felt urgency of repurposing and revamping higher education in the country by rejuvenating our languishing university system to enable smooth navigation through the challenges of the 21st century that stare at us on account of knowledge explosion, digital revolution, and the unforeseen pandemic triggering current disruptions. The well-crafted narrative provides wholesome insights into the key issues of governance and leadership within the existing framework through practical suggestions on academic, administration, and fiscal reforms. The book also underscores the point that our HEIs need new, imaginative, and sustainable governance architecture to become globally competitive, effectively implement NEP-2020, restructure academic offerings in real-time, and restore primacy of research and creative pursuits. It rightly emphasizes the pivotal role of quality in higher education and elaborates on the role of regulatory and ranking bodies in promoting quality education and research. The author makes a fervent appeal for the disengagement of regulatory bodies from controlling universities and allowing them the freedom to innovate in the teaching-learning processes and experiment with emerging ideas and trends to build their own brands. This chronicle on universities is well conceived, topical, and laced with pragmatism. It articulates well on what can be and should be done in near term, and, it can very well serve as a 'Coffee Table' book for academicians, vice chancellors, policy makers (of both state and federal government), regulatory bodies, and all those interested and committed to the advance of our higher education system.

Prof. Goverdhan Mehta, FNA, FRS,
Former Vice Chancellor, Central University of Hyderabad
and Director, IISc., Bengaluru.

'Remodeling the Universities' delineates excellent thought process to pen down for the benefit of HEIs in the light of NEP-2020. The author's thoughts on the 'leadership and governance' with examples for delegation of powers and, reflections on the advances in *the third* wave of internet, AI and Machine learning, the unforeseen COVID-19, and online platforms of education are well expounded. Ideas on redesigning the 'Centers of Human Resource Development', undertaking administrative reforms and role of accrediting bodies and State Higher Education Councils in ushering both transactional and transformational reforms in universities/colleges are very thoughtful and facilitative in smooth implementation of NEP-2020 in the country. Management of fiscal resources, contextualizing the content and delivery of curriculum, and promotion of germane research with 'User-Friendly Guidelines for Operation of Research Grants' as an addendum are an impetus to the academia. The book is a must read for teaching faculty and administrators of HEIs.

Prof. S.C. Sharma

Director, National Assessment and Accreditation Council (NAAC), Nagarabhavi, Bengaluru.

'Remodeling the Universities' is a timely reminder of challenges awaiting the implementation of the NEP-2020. The focus is on higher education in 'pursuit of higher objectives of life and truth'. The vastly experienced author has comprehensively discussed regulatory bodies and their infringement on academic autonomy, infrastructure needs, effective integration of interdisciplinary courses and innovative curriculum design, rampant politicization, and above all, faculty-quality in the face of massive inbreeding.

Prof. Sushanta Dattagupta, FNA

Former Vice Chancellor, Visva Bharati University, Santiniketan (WB), and Founder Director, IISER, Kolkata.

With the declaration of NEP-2020, the challenges confronted by the education policy thinkers have become intense. In this context, this volume on *'Remodeling the Universities'* has not only come at appropriate time but also deals with many in-depth issues from the lens of a world known scientist, and a very successful Vice Chancellor of one of the best universities in the country. Prof. Saidapur analyses history of education and the emergence of university system to proceed further with his rich experience on leadership in administration, finances, contextualizing the research along with curricula and relationship with conglomerated colleges. The book delves inherently most of the themes of NEP-2020 that run under the crest of this implementable analytical volume.

Prof. R.S. Deshpande, FISAE,
ICSSR National Fellow Former Director 'Institute for Social and Economic Change' (ISEC), Nagarabhavi, Bengaluru.

This is an excellent and comprehensive analysis of what is wrong in our Higher Education System. New insights have been provided on every dimension of higher education keeping in mind the drawbacks of the current system and repurposing of the system for future needs. Prof. Saidapur's vast experience as a scientist, as a teacher par excellence, as an educationist, and as an able academic administrator with a vision has shaped the opinions expressed in this book. I think that this book should be read along with the NEP-2020 document of Dr. K. Kasturirangan committee to understand the significance of reforms suggested and the depth and width of understanding the vast and complex higher education system of our country with over 1000 universities and 40000 colleges. Of course, being a decorated scientist of our country, he has focused on science education in more detail than Humanities and Social sciences. This book calls for a new classification of human knowledge demanding parallel action in designing new courses, departments, and centres. The author recommends an organic and purposeful growth of our campuses avoiding repetitive and non-innovative cancerous growth of knowledge domains witnessed hitherto. This book is a must read for all faculty already in service and for those who are yet to be recruited.

Prof. K. Muralidhar, FNA,
Former Head, Department of Zoology, University of Delhi, Sir J. C. Bose national Fellow, South Asian University, New Delhi, and Jawaharlal Nehru Chair, School of Life Sciences, University of Hyderabad, Hyderabad.

Acknowledgements

My grateful thanks are to Prof. Basavaraj G. Mulimani, former Vice Chancellor, Gulbarga University, Kalaburgi, and BLDE Medical University, Vijayapura (Karnataka), whose loving friendship I happen to enjoy during the past 50 years and with whom I had numerous informal conversations which often helped me to see the other side of the coin and think differently. Unsurprisingly, these ideas are unwittingly embedded in this book.

I thank Prof. Bhagyashri A. Shanbhag, my former colleague at Karnatak University, for reading the draft, giving helpful suggestions, and spotting typos which helped me in polishing the script.

I am very much indebted to Prof. Goverdhan Mehta, Prof. R.S. Deshpande, Prof. S.C. Sharma, Prof. Sushanta Dattagupta, and Prof. K. Muralidhar for not only providing many valuable suggestions on the draft manuscript but also for scripting their opinions on the book.

Finally, I thank with great pleasure M/s Atlantic Publishers & Distributors Pvt. Ltd., New Delhi, for gladly undertaking the publication of this book and extending cooperation at various steps of its publication.

Prof. Srinivas K. Saidapur

Preface

Higher Education commonly refers to undergraduate (UG) and postgraduate (PG) level of studies. The term 'higher' has also a deeper meaning; it refers to the pursuit of higher objectives of life and search of truth. In India, the universities to which various colleges in the region are affiliated oversee the management of higher education. In turn, the regulatory bodies like the UGC, AICTE, ICAR, BCI, MCI, and others control the universities through certain regulations. Ideally, such regulatory bodies should provide novel ideas and leadership to universities to produce quality human resource to meet the challenges of changing global scenario and the current and future needs in diverse fields of human endeavours—progresses in the field of science and technology, economy of the country, healthcare systems, defence systems, managing international affairs, sustainable use of environmental resources, and importantly, the challenges arising out of demographic changes (the segments of populations broken by age, sex or income). Finally, living in harmony depends on the quality of human resource and education. Universities are the sites where skilled and competent men with noble values are shaped. Therefore, wellbeing of a nation rests largely on the performance of its universities.

The past several decades have witnessed fragmentation of many disciplines (both in science and social sciences) giving rise to numerous sub disciplines that have grown remarkably and in the process generated much needed new knowledge. However, such fragmentation has impeded conceptualization and consolidation of the basic subject domains. A deeper grasp of intricacies, fundamentals, and conceptualization depend upon integration (judicious mix) of knowledge derived from sub disciplines and other areas. Fittingly, therefore, the National Education

Policy-2020 advocates integration of related subject domains that have more or less lost their borders. A major challenge of universities now pertains to restructuring and repurposing the teaching and research programs. Universities need to evolve new courses through integration of not only the sub disciplines but also different disciplines and pave way for multidisciplinary approach in research. In brief, universities need to initiate steps—to redesign teaching-learning-assessment pedagogies, for preparation of context and outcome based curriculums, and for promotion of relevant research, creativity, and innovation. With such challenges in mind, the book strives to provide insights for remodeling the universities. It urges for reorganization of governance processes, highlights significance of enlightened leadership role of Vice Chancellors, need for contextualizing the curriculums, promotion of germane research, recognizing the transformative value of the *third wave of internet* on education, roles of Human Resource Development Centres (HRDCs), State Higher Education Councils (SHECs), and National Assessment and Accreditation Council (NAAC), and so on in the resurrection of higher education.

Finally, the book ends with reflections on the future of higher education and universities, and a postscript based on the author's long sojourn with the varsity education.

Prof. Srinivas K. Saidapur

Abbreviations

AA	Alumni Association
AC	Academic Council
AI	Artificial Intelligence
AICTE	All India Council of Technical Education
API	Academic Performance Index
BCI	Bar Council of India
BOG	Board of Governors
BOM	Board of Management
BOS	Board of Studies
BSR	Basic Science Research
CEO	Chief Executive Officer
CIC	Centre for Industry Collaboration
COD	Chairperson of the Department
CBCS	Choice Based Credit System
CSIR	Council of Scientific and Industrial Research
CSR	Corporate Social Responsibility
DBT	Department of Biotechnology
DOE	Department of Environment
DST	Department of Science and Technology
E	Education
EC	Executive Council
ECCE	Early Childhood Care Education
Gen-Z	Persons born between 1990-2010
HEI	Higher Education Institution

HRDC	Human Resource Development Centre
ICAR	Indian Council of Agricultural Research
ICMR	Indian Council of Medical Research
ICSSR	Indian Council of Social Science Research
ICT	Information Communication Technology
IIIT	Indian Institute of Information Technology
IIM	Indian Institute of Management
IISc	Indian Institute of Science
IISER	Indian Institute for Science Education and Research
IoT	Internet of Things
IQAC	Internal Quality Assurance Cell
IR	Industrial Revolution
ISEC	Institute for Social and Economic Change
KSTA	Karnataka Science and Technology Academy
LIC	Local Inquiry Committee
MCI	Medical Council of India
MHRD	Ministry of Human Resource Development
MOOC	Massive Open Online Courseware
MOE	Ministry of Education (Earlier called MHRD)
MOU	Memorandum of Understanding
NAAC	National Assessment and Accreditation Council
NBA	National Board of Accreditation
NEP	National Education Policy
NET	National Eligibility Test
NIRF	National Institutional Ranking Framework
NISER	National Institute of Science Education and Research
NIIT	National Institute of Information Technology
OC	Orientation Course
PISA	Program for International Student Assessment

PMB	Planning and Monitoring Body
PPP	Public Private Partnership
QnM	Quantitative Metrics
QlM	Qualitative Metrics
R&D	Research and Development
RC	Refresher Course
RUSA	Rashtriya Uchhatara Shiksha Abhiyan
SHEC	State Higher Education Council
UEIGB	University Employment Information Guidance Bureau
UGC	University Grants Commission
USIC	University Science Instrumentation Centre

Contents

Chapter 1

Historical Perspectives on the Indian Universities: A Run-up

> *A university stands for humanism, for tolerance, for reason, for the adventure of ideas and for the search of truth. It stands for the onward march of the human race towards even higher objectives. If the universities discharge their duties adequately, then it is well with the Nation and the people.*
>
> —Jawaharlal Nehru

The above quote is an eminent assertion of the significance of higher education and the central role of universities in building a civilized society that is worth inhabiting. This chapter is to recapitulate the major landmarks in the establishment and progression of higher education systems in India. Knowledge of historical developments in any field is essential. The history of Indian education is quite interesting. It was closely linked with sages, saints, revered Gurus in the ancient times, and the rulers (in particular, the British). The *Gurukul* (Hindu Residential School) system practiced from the ancient times, before the first millennium i.e. before the beginning of the Common Era/Christian Era (BCE) is in vogue even today in isolated pockets of India and also overseas. The *Gurukul* system of education was typically practiced in hermitages or 'Ashrams' providing knowledge on diverse subjects like literature, ancient scriptures, history, herbal medicine, astrology, astronomy, warfare, archery, statesmanship, philosophy, religion, spirituality and so on. During their stay in the 'Ashram', the *shishyas* (pupils) invariably rendered variety of services like the household chores and served the Guru (teacher) with great reverence and dedication. The services rendered by the learners were in a way a part of education process. Based on the competency, attainment of knowledge and skills by the learners, the Guru would declare their readiness to leave his Ashram. He would then give a ritualized sermon to the trainees on how to lead a good life with due regard to code of conduct, practice of moral and ethical values and so on before bidding them farewell; the modern-day convocations are equivalent to such sermons. The learners would then return to their homes after paying their respect and *Gurudakshina* (honorarium) to their Guru and respects to his spouse, the *Gurumata* (the mother teacher).

In Sanskrit language, teachers are grouped into six types: *Adhyapak* (one who gives information), *Upadhaya* (one who gives knowledge), *Acharya* (one who imparts skills-recall Dronacharya of Mahabharat), *Pandit* (one who provides deep insight in the subject), *Dhrista* (one who provides visionary view), and *Guru* (who awakens wisdom leading from darkness to light). Incidentally, these six terms used to describe teachers depict a deeper meaning of *Gurukul* system of education and richness of Sanskrit language. The modern-day designations like the assistant professor, associate professor, and professor hardly match the terminologies used in the ancient India before the start of the Common Era/Christian Era (CE). Considering their richness, Sanskrit and Pali languages clearly need revival and nurturing to reap rich dividends from ancient scriptures and texts written in these languages. To consider *Sanskrit* as a dead language is more out of our ignorance than realism.

It is widely believed that before the 8th century, in the first millennium, India already had a vibrant education system, with highly reputed knowledge imparting centres often regarded as the universities. Prominent among these were located in Nalanda (Bihar), Takshashila (also referred as Taxila, now in Rawalpindi, Pakistan), Ujjain (Madhya Pradesh), Vikramshila (Bhagalpur, Bihar), Odantapuri (Bihar Sharif, Bihar), Jagaddala, Somapura Naogaon (now in Bangladesh), Valabhi (Bhavnagar, Gujarat), Pushpagiri (Jeypore District of Odisha), and Ratnagiri (Maharashtra). These centres provided education to good number of scholars from different countries and these were thus well-known internationally. Other very eminent study centres include the 'Sharada Peeth' in Kashmir and Kanchipuram in Tamil Nadu. The above centres of learning taught diverse subjects like the Art, Archery, Architecture, Arthashastra (Economics), Astronomy (particularly in Ujjain), Buddhism, Hinduism, Herbal Medicine (particularly in Takshashila), Judiciary (ranging from family court to King's court), Painting and so on. Attraction of students from many foreign countries plainly depicts the magnificence of these institutions in the bygone era. The Nalanda University being the biggest education hub seems to have housed as many as 10,000 students during its glorious days. The University of Takshashila now in Pakistan represents the world's first university. Unfortunately, these institutions are now in ruins and left to themselves to remain as relics and despondently remind us of their past glory. By the end of seventeenth century, education was widespread with schools in temples (*Pathashalas*), mosques (*Madrasas*) or townships in many parts of the Indian continent. The *Pathashalas* were generally engaged in teaching mathematics, astronomy, law, medicine, religion, spirituality, and also metaphysics.

Before the mid-nineteenth century, learners had only a modest access to books and libraries. The knowledge, and resources in the form of Vedas, Upanishads, Puranas, Smrutis (recollections based on human memory) and Shrutis (based on what is heard), epics like *Ramayana* and *Mahabharata*, Panini's *Ashtadyayi*, Kautilya's *Arthashastra* (dated 322-298 BCE), Bharata's *Natyashastra*, Medical treatises of Chakra and Sushruta, Dramas of Shudraka, Bhasa, Kalidasa, teachings of Buddha, Mahaveera and others from different regions of the Indian continent were however available. Teaching-learning processes may have been more passive than active in ancient India involving chiefly transfer of knowledge from the teacher and passive absorption by the learner. Yet, fierce discussions and debates also took place between the eminent scholars on matters of fundamental and ultimate truths (God, 'Dvaita and Advaita' philosophy, etc.). The classic example involves the much discussed and the classic debate between Sri Adi Shankara and Mandana Mishra involving a fundamental issue pertaining to *Atman and Brahman*—to arrive at a conclusion as to whether they are (one and) the same or two different entities. Interestingly, India is one rare country, which has produced large number of erudite philosophers and saints, a noteworthy feature. Importantly, science also has its origins in philosophy. In fact, it is the starting point of logic and in turn of scientific developments. Undeniably, one can see and admire certain scientific developments in the Indian continent in the bygone era. These are evident in the area of Mathematics, Astronomy, Ayurveda, Metallurgy, Temple Architecture and so on. One should recall contributions of Aryabhata (550-476 CE), Varahamihira (587-505 CE), Brahmagupta (668-598 CE), Bhaskara-I (680-600 CE), and the 12th century mathematician and astronomer the Bhaskaracharya (1185-1114 CE) also called Bhaskara-II (from Bijapur now renamed as Vijayapura in Karnataka) to avoid confusion, and his famous treatise on mathematics called Leelavati. The golden age of Indian medicine, the 'Ayurveda' reigned from 800 BC to about 1000 CE which produced two major treatises known as 'Charaka Samhita' and 'Sushruta Samhita'. Charaka was a physician and Sushruta was a surgeon. Charaka is regarded as the Indian Father of Medicine. Similarly, advances in metallurgy and temple architecture in ancient India depict progresses in diverse fields of science and engineering. However, in eulogising our scientific development, some caution is needed. The various legendary depictions such as those encountered in the epics of *Ramayana*, *Mahabharata*, and in the ancient literature may not represent true scientific advancements; they however depict fertile mind (creativity and innovation in today's parlance) and power of imagination of our ancestors.

Now let us come to the modern education system that was initiated in the late nineteenth century. As the East India Company that had spread its tentacles of business network in most parts of India, needed people to interpret between them and the natives to facilitate day-to-day communication and promote trade. This led the British Government to take initiatives to 'civilize the natives' through western education and create a class of people who could handily serve as interpreters between the government and the masses as well as carryout numerous everyday tasks. This was possible only by training the natives in the use of English medium, and adoption of English customs and mannerisms. Accordingly, Sir T.B. Macaulay (1835) recommended to the British Government to provide English education to the native Indians so as to "to create, a class who would be interpreters between us and the millions whom we govern, a class of persons, Indian in blood and colour, but English in tastes, in opinions, in moral and in intellect, who would be consumers of British goods, provide recruits for the subordinate ranks of the East India Company's civil service and be loyal to the Raj". Creating such a class of Indians was essentially to serve the British as their loyal subordinates. Furthermore, adoption of English as medium of instruction helped in teaching British History and its glory. In addition, it facilitated the missionaries to preach and spread Christianity. The credit of sowing seeds of Western education in English language goes to both Sir Charles Wood (recall the famed 'Wood's Dispatch') and Sir Macaulay. Thus began the journey of modern and formal education in India around the mid-nineteenth century. At the same time, it also heralded progressive destruction and disrespect for the indigenous knowledge, culture, lifestyles, local languages, especially the Sanskrit. Soon, the psyche of natives also changed resulting in spitefulness for Indian culture, and reverence for English culture and foreign commodities. The greatest consequence of this was driving the attributes like wisdom enshrined in ancient scriptures (in the form of Vedas, Upanishads, and Epics, etc.), acumen of Kautilya's *Arthashastra*, Vedic mathematics, Astronomy, Ayurveda, Architecture, Yoga and Meditation, significance of spiritual knowledge and so on to oblivion. Further, the unfortunate fallout of Macaulay's doctrine was loss of self-esteem in the minds of natives. This is a great blow that still haunts us; killing self-esteem is killing overall development of people and human society, and in turn the nation.

The establishment of formal institutions of higher education, the colleges, and the universities in India began during the colonial days. Thyagarajan (2019) has recently described the progression of higher education systems from colonial days to the modern times. Briefly, the first important step was the 'Wood's Dispatch' (1854) which heralded the establishment of Universities in Calcutta (now Kolkata), Bombay (now Mumbai) and Madras (now Chennai) on the lines of London University in 1857. This paved way for subsequent establishment and expansion of higher education through the 'Indian Universities (Degree) Act' enacted in 1860, which led to the setting up of colleges in different regions of the country. These eventually became universities [e.g. Lahore (now in Pakistan), Allahabad (now Prayagraj), and Aligarh, etc.]. The Punjab University was then established in 1882, Banaras Hindu University and University of Mysore in 1916, Osmania University in 1918, Aligarh Muslim University in 1920, all before the country got its independence from the British rule. By 1947 (the year of independence) India had 19 universities and around 500 degree colleges. The number of colleges and universities increased progressively with time but the rise in their number in the past few decades is phenomenal. For instance, as of now, there are as many as 911 universities and 41,900 colleges. Further, new Central and State universities and institutions like the IISERs, NISERs, IITs, IIITs and NIITs continue to be established from time to time. The intention of creating such institutions is good. However, the political considerations generally goad the governments in power to create such institutions in remote, not easily accessible areas (e.g. Rajiv Gandhi University in Itanagar, Arunachal Pradesh, Central University in Koraput in Orissa, IITs in Mandi, Ropar and so on). We also hear about the possible establishment of an IISER in Nagaland. Bringing education to under-privileged corners of the country is laudable. However, soon the fallacy may surface to the fore, as it is very difficult to attract a reasonably good faculty to such remote areas. Often the faculty from local colleges and universities end up securing jobs in such supposedly premier institutions. Even in Shillong (Meghalaya) a relatively cosmopolitan city, a Central University—the North Eastern Hill University (NEHU) could not sustain what started out to be a promising pan-India university. A similar fate seems to have befallen the IISER in Berhampur, Orissa and some newly established Central Universities. An unintended consequence of creating Central Universities and IISERs is deprivation of State universities from getting good faculty, good students, and decent funding. Impoverishment of the traditional universities of the State (that offer diverse courses of great importance) is disastrous as they cater to the major chunk of student population. Therefore, both the State and Central Governments must first strive to strengthen the existing State varsities to raise them to the level of the Central Universities in all respects by creating mechanisms and policies for recruitment of competent faculty, decent funding, and improving service conditions, on par with the Central varsities.

Clearly, the premier science institutions like the IITs, IISERs, NISERs, NIITs, IISc, are not the substitutes for traditional universities that have all disciplines including the social sciences, liberal arts, and fine arts under the same umbrella along with pure science or technology and a stated or unstated mandate of catering largely to the local and regional needs. Further, the traditional universities have great potential for providing education in liberal arts. A component of liberal arts is very important in all streams of education. The phrase *liberal arts* coined in the 8th century BCE includes subjects or skills like the logic, rhetoric or oratory, arithmetic, geometry, music, astronomy and even grammar. In Greek, "liberalis" means "free" and "arts" means "principled practice". In recent times, scope of liberal arts, is expanded to include "fine arts"—various creative activities like painting, sculpture, architecture, music (composition and performance), singing, dance, drama, poetry, and literature. Thus, there is always an overlap between liberal arts and fine arts. The study of liberal arts is considered essential to the well-educated persons in the western world to enable them to participate in civic life. In short, study of liberal arts helps in creating all rounded personality. One may ask, is there any scientific perspective to this? Yes there is. From a scientific perspective, human brain is distinguishable as *left-half* and a *right-half*; these are anatomically identical but functionally different. A well-developed left-brain (functionally) is typical of people who are more logical, analytical, and theoretical, the common attributes of lawyers, police officers, detectives, chartered accountants and so on. On the other hand, a (functionally) well-developed right-brain is typical of people endowed with ability for creativeness, artistic nature, feeling of strong emotions as seen in people who are writers, poets or artists (singers, musicians, sculptors, painters, dancers and so on). The twenty-first century education demands creativity and critical thinking. Therefore, in ensuring a balanced development of right and left hemispheres of the brain, study of liberal arts can help greatly. Hence, the study of liberal arts during graduation courses is thus very important for students of all streams including the professional ones. However, for most people, a balance between the left and the right-brain is desirable.

The various education institutions of higher learning especially the universities differ with each other considerably in their structure, organization and governance: Affiliating, Residential, Multi-faculty, Mono-faculty (e.g. Language, Folklore, Law, Engineering, Medical, and Dental etc.), Central, State or Private Universities (with or without State funding), institutions of national importance with 'Deemed University' status, 'Women's Universities' and so on. Thus, all universities with the exception of a few (e.g. Banaras Hindu University, Aligarh Muslim University and Visva Bharati University) were established with British mold. Therefore, one wonders how a self-respecting country like India stands to gain by decoupling from its past heritage and at the same time hope to flourish by incorporating foreign values and practices at the cost of long cherished indigenous values and customs!

Soon after independence in the year 1947, India needed a roadmap for espousal and expansion of higher education through establishment of colleges and universities, and mechanisms for their general uniform operation across the country. Accordingly, an education commission was setup under the Chairmanship of the most eminent scholar of the time, Sir Sarvepalli Radhakrishnan, an internationally renowned philosopher, professor, diplomat, and administrator to prepare a roadmap of higher education. The report of Radhakrishnan Commission "Indian University Education Commission" (1948-49) continues to be the fundamental and guiding force for all subsequent education commissions that include: Kothari Commission (1964-66), Knowledge Commission of India (2005-09), Yashpal Committee (2008-09), and Kasturirangan Committee (2020) inter alia; these reports are succinctly summarized recently (Shanbhag, 2019a). Sadly, the above reports found only partial implementation and the ideas provided therein were not fully made use of.

A piecemeal approach does not yield desired results. Ideally, recommendations of the various Commission reports, especially that of S. Radhakrishnan, and D.S. Kothari should have been implemented fully, and introspected periodically and incorporate corrective measures as well as new ideas relevant for overall national growth and development. This would have helped us avoid the present mess with respect to the implementation of NEP 2020. Frequent changes in policies pose numerous problems for students, teachers, and implementers. Ideally, the education system should remain in dynamic state and keep refining from time to time as per the contemporaneous needs.

The very idea of a university, its prime goals, and different dimensions of higher education like academic freedom, university as a site of resistance and so on are discussed and debated widely; the literature is replete with such discussions and noteworthy deliberations (Chandra 2017; Pathania 2018; Saidapur 2019a; Varghese et al., 2019). The trends in the twenty-first century education and role of teachers were also described recently (Saidapur 2020abc). Let us ask, what are the basic objectives of a university? In simple terms, a university is a place that provides for universal education with a scope for free thinking, generating new ideas and for inspired pursuit of truth. In India, scholars and thinkers like Sri Aurobindo, Vivekananda, Rabindranath Tagore, Sarvepalli Radhakrishnan and Jawaharlal Nehru and others have commented on the significance of (higher) education and universities. Nehru opined that if the universities discharge their duties adequately, then it is well with the nation and the people. Therefore, the expectations of the society from higher centres of learning, principally the universities will always remain very high as far as the national development and progression, and production of worthy human resource is concerned. Undeniably, quality education is a prerequisite for building good human resource, which in turn ensures development of human societies, and progresses in science and technology base as well as the 'economic growth' of the nation. At the same time, building a humanistic society requires inculcation of moral, ethical, and spiritual values and patriotism. Unmistakably, human societies evolve largely based on the strength and quality of higher education. Hence, education programs should serve to inspire tolerance of different religious faiths and beliefs and pursuit of truth. In fact, inculcation of cultures and attributes like the benevolence constitute the major objectives of *higher* education. Thus, if all is not well with the society today, it only means that all is not well with the universities. As a matter of fact, human behaviour especially during the testing times like the pandemics, catastrophes like deluge, earth quakes, and fires and so on reflect quality of education imparted in the country. Further, even in normal times, people's behaviour on the streets (spitting, littering, and attending to nature's calls, violating traffic norms, etc.) and shopping malls deafeningly reflect quality of education imparted to the citizens.

Apart from providing basic education in diverse fields, the universities are expected to provide leadership to the country through research, development, novel ideas and competent expert manpower in diverse fields so as to enhance overall quality of life, prosperity, good international relations, true spiritualism and happiness of the society. The twenty-first century demands good focus on promoting critical and creative thinking, making innovations and acquisition of skills, and prepare learners who will be future ready and add value to the positions they occupy or vocations they undertake. Furthermore, with the massive impact of the *third wave* of internet (internet of everything) and 'app-based' economy, citizens of all countries aspire for a global citizenship. Thus, higher education should not only address to resolving local and national problems but also the global challenges. In order to accomplish these objectives, universities need academic freedom, first rate faculty, generous financial support, and freedom from political interferences. At the same time, universities must remain accountable for their performance, contribution, and existence as the public money supports them.

In any discussion on 'literacy' and 'education', often we fail to understand the tacit meanings of these terms. The terms 'literacy' and 'education' are not synonymous to each other. There is a difference between being *literate* and *educated*. A literate person knows how to read and write. Whereas, an educated person knows how to behave in normal and difficult times with concerns for fellow human beings, and the environment in which she/he lives. Literacy by itself does not make a person educated but it is a fine tool to transform oneself and become inspired to pursue higher knowledge about anything that matters-meaning of life to significance of spirituality. Sri Aurobindo opined that education is largely the training of the mind, body, and soul. Only a good education can help transform a person through acquired knowledge and skills and shape her/his behaviour and development of fine human qualities. In the end it should promote all-round advancement of the society and peaceful existence of man with all living beings. The prime objective of *higher* education is thus to gain knowledge and wisdom which in turn leads a person towards the pursuit of truth and higher objectives of life that is, search for meaning and purpose of life (philosophical and metaphysical aspects). Historically therefore teachers constituted the most revered segment of the society. In India value of teachers was recognized since Vedic times (Bronze age of India; c. 1500 – c. 1100 BCE) as eminently described in a Sanskrit verse: *Gurur Brahma, Gurur Vishnu, Gurur Devo Maheshwara, Gurur Sakshat Parabrahma, Tasmai Shree Guruve Namah*. Translated, the verse means: a teacher is like Lord Brahma the creator who generates knowledge within us; like Lord Vishnu the preserver who drives ideas and knowledge into our mind; and like Lord Maheshwara the destroyer of ill-conceived ideas and help us stay on the right path and enlightened. To such a Guru we offer our salutations. An ideal teacher is therefore (1) a creator of knowledge, (2) preserver of knowledge thus created, and (3) destroyer of evil thoughts in the minds of his pupils. Teaching is therefore a noble profession. Additionally, sensitizing learners about the importance of honesty, integrity in day-to-day life, spirit of patriotism, tolerance towards fellow citizens, gender equality, respect, and empathy for elders and, citizenry are important components of education. It is in this process, the universities and teachers have a key role to play (Saidapur, 2020b).

Anyone will value the importance of good education. However, often we fail to visualize the impact of bad education and bad practices in education institutions. The statement of late Nelson Mandela (President of South Africa) flaunted at the

University of South Africa elegantly summarizes the implications of bad education. It says, "Collapsing any nation does not require use of atomic bombs or the use of long-range missiles. It only requires lowering the quality of education and allowing cheating in the examinations by the students." The following lines further emphasize the same: "The patient dies in the hands of the doctor who passed his exams through cheating. The buildings collapse in the hands of an engineer who passed his exams through cheating. The money is lost in the hands of an accountant who passed his exams through cheating. Humanity dies in the hands of a religious scholar who passed his exams through cheating. Justice is lost in the hands of a judge who passed his exams through cheating. Ignorance is rampant in the minds of children who are under the care of a teacher who passed exams through cheating. Collapse of education is collapse of the nation" (*source*: Google). Later, Prosper Dzitse wrote in his blog: "Shoddy laws are made by the politician who passed exams through cheating. Half or unverified information is given by the journalist who passed exams through cheating. Unjustifiable/unpatriotic actions are supported by citizens who passed exams through cheating. Substandard works are done by the public/civil servant who passed exams through cheating. Half/subjective analysis is given by civil society organizations whose leaders passed exams through cheating. Uninspiring leadership is given by the leader who passed exams through cheating. Indeed, the collapse of education is the collapse of the Nation" (*source*: Google). These statements coming from South Africa aptly describe the on-going scenario of higher education in several countries. They require no further explanation.

Radically thinking and liberal minded intellectuals often suggest that the universities besides carrying out routine teaching and research should also become sites for resistance against unjust inequitable policies of the ruling governments. The idea is fine as long as the faculty members do not involve in real-time politics and take sides either in favour or against the government based on the political ideologies. The universities should not become breeding grounds for future political parties and promotion of mediocrity. Decades of experience shows that

Teachers' Associations generally fight for easy promotions and increase in salary. They rarely resist against bad governance, appointment of mediocre faculty and incompetent vice chancellors, and political interferences. Likewise, they rarely raise voice for improvement of infrastructure, creating vibrant academic ecosystem, student amenities, building institutional cultures, contextualizing curriculum to meet societal needs, modernizing pedagogies, providing academic flexibility and so on. The academic community has all the moral obligation to channelize its energy to help evolve (1) a better education system, (2) policies for the State and the Nation (foreign affairs, trade, etc.), (3) streamlining institutional and the State Government governance, (4) promotion of religious harmony, (5) protection of biodiversity and environment, (6) prevention of pollution, (7) improvement of economy, trade, tourism, and (8) tackling local, regional, national and global challenges (e.g. changing demographic scenario) and so on. The concept of liberalism and universities as the sites of resistance will make sense if it contributes to visible improvements in managing the affairs of institutions both at the State and the National levels. Certainly, academicians must strive to shape the nation and actively participate in formulating policies and their implementation. But, they should remain free from politics and party affiliations so as to be effective and credible.

An important dimension of education is that there exists a close link between Education (E) and Industrial Revolutions (IRs). Educational progresses, research in science and technology and IRs are interrelated and greatly affect each other. Thus far four major IRs have taken place (IR 1.0-IR 4.0). The IR 1.0 took place in England around the year 1780 CE. This was the *Textile Revolution* enabled by 'Mechanization' of productions using water, steam power and weaving looms. The cotton and coal required to herald IR 1.0 went to UK mostly from India. The IR 2.0 occurred a century later in the USA (around the year 1870 CE) using electricity that enabled 'Mass Production' using assembly lines. The IR 3.0 characterized by 'Automation' was due to progresses in electronics and simple digital technology around the year 1969 CE. The first three IRs are spaced by approximately a century. However, the IR 4.0 was accomplished in less than 20 years after the IR 3.0 due to the development of complex digital technology (using Cyber Physical Systems) that enabled use of robots, 3-D printing, quantum computing, artificial intelligence (AI), complex networking called internet of things (IoT), etc. The world is now witnessing the *third wave of internet* called '*Internet of Everything*'. Now let us ask, how has the Indian education system evolved over the centuries? Briefly, it has progressed from E 1.0-E 4.0 in parallel to the four IRs. The *Gurukul* system represents E 1.0 that involved use of traditional methods of teaching where the Guru signified the total embodiment of knowledge and little access to formal libraries. This system dominated from time immemorial. The E 2.0 began around the mid-twentieth century marking transition from passive to active learning, e-learning, collaborations with other institutions, and open access to teaching-learning resources and furtherance of research, thanks to internet facility. The digital technologies also helped in the management of governance and teaching-learning-evaluation processes more effectively. The E 3.0 encompasses use of integrated approach of technology with teaching-learning processes: a confluence of neuroscience, cognitive psychology, education technology, web-based digital and mobile technologies (apps, hardware, software, etc.). Whereas, a major concern of E 4.0 is to draw a blueprint for future education (Saidapur 2019d). Accordingly, India is now gearing up to implement the "National Education Policy 2020" (NEP 2020) which presents a great hope and a long-awaited opportunity for revamping the country's education system as a whole—from schools to universities.

As with any new initiative the NEP 2020 poses many challenges in its implementation. Major challenges include assimilating the core philosophy of NEP 2020, making all needed logistic preparations, creating new infrastructure, integration of borderless sub-disciplines, evolving new course structures with progressive complexities and continuity of thoughts, modernizing teaching-learning-assessment processes, changing the mind-set of teachers and stakeholders, and substantial investments on the part of governments and private players. Logistic challenges include maintaining credits earned by each student with authenticity across numerous institutions, and developing smooth mechanisms for their transfer when needed. The need to complete 50% of curriculum within the degree granting institution can limit mobility between institutions. Multiple exit and entry options also create many logistic problems when it comes to admitting students of any institution to any other institution across the States. A related issue pertains to the employability of dropouts with myriads of certificates/diploma. If such dropouts become unemployable, the institutions issuing such certificates will lose their credentials and the certifications lose the credibility. Poor Faculty-Student Ratio (FSR) and paucity of funds are sure to pose serious problems. Academic bureaucracy in India is not user-friendly either. All said and done, implementation of recommendations in letter and spirit is crucial for making NEP 2020 successful.

In the past, recommendations of various education commissions and committees were only partially implemented. If the same fate befalls on the NEP 2020, it will result in a missed opportunity; a too costly affair to which future generations are unlikely to pardon. What the NEP proposes for higher education, and why is it so important? Short answers for these questions are as follows. The on-going IR 4.0 has massive effects in terms of both speed and impact. Visible impacts are the *technology driven disruptions in jobs* (various types). Classic example is Kodak Eastman Company; the world's largest film-making company, which once had ~170,000 employees, is now bankrupt and all employees lost their jobs. With every passing decade 40-50 types of jobs are becoming obsolete and vanishing. Fortunately, new jobs are also created which however require new skills. The recent outbreak of Covid-19 which revealed the importance of social and personal hygiene also promoted online activity in every aspect of human life (e.g. holding online meetings and webinars, coaching, conducting online classes—schools to universities, various businesses including home delivery of groceries, food, and medicines etc.) that included common man and children. In short, now more than ever learning skills, developing ability for critical and creative thinking, and making innovations have become inevitable. All this means, learning, unlearning and relearning are the basic tenets of education today. Importance of these maxims is well depicted by Alvin Toffler who said, "The illiterates of the 21st century will not be those who cannot read and write but those who cannot learn, unlearn and relearn". In addition, life-long learning should become part of life. Relevance of the NEP 2020 lies in recognizing the concerns cited above and other on-going national and global challenges. A biggest challenge that impedes successful implementation of NEP 2020 is the absence of competent faculty in sufficient numbers in all educational institutions. Added to this is the near absence of enlightened and competent leadership at almost all levels in the hierarchy of higher education institutions.

To sum up, education is the central organizing principle in the evolution of human societies and the nation in which the universities have a key role to play. In India, universities set up around the time of country's independence strived hard and earned good reputation by establishing basic infrastructure in accordance with the given point of time, and also imparted quality education. Interestingly, that was the period when not many competent personnel were available locally for various faculty positions. But, the universities had freedom to invite well qualified faculty from different parts of India and abroad (non-resident Indian scholars). Accordingly, the vice chancellors exercised this privilege, invited, and appointed worthy faculty from all over the country that sustained initial development of varsities. Apparently, this was possible because the universities then enjoyed autonomy and were free from political interferences. The various postgraduate (PG) departments then began taking shape placing the teaching program on a firm footing. Under the guidance of good faculty drawn from different parts of the country, the local students began getting PG and doctoral degrees (Ph.D.). Soon thereafter, some students secured scholarships to go abroad for postdoctoral research and earned additional experience and qualification. This enabled them to secure faculty positions, often in their own alma mater which added to their happiness. The new faculty members (of local origin) also worked hard to become good teachers and researchers as they were competing with their own former teachers and other colleagues representing pan India. Hence, these local (and hence inbred) faculty members had a purpose and commitment to prove their worth. As the years rolled on the recruitment of faculty mostly got confined to local personnel due to their availability, aspirations and for political reasons. Over the time, this has led to a massive inbreeding and loss of hybrid vigour. Consequently, teaching and research activities became routine and uninspiring. Further, the universities rarely (or poorly) addressed the issue of obsolescence of the learners in tackling diverse problems, and overall ability to solve new challenges based on the training imparted to them at UG/PG courses. Astonishingly, Dr. Vikram Sarabhai, the great visionary recognized the issue of obsolescence of learners long ago. In his Convocation Address at IIT Madras (1968), Sarabhai said, "In nature, left to itself, control is maintained through an ecological balance. Order is not imposed from above, but arises through the interaction of each unit with its environment in a dynamic equilibrium. On the other hand, inherent in a program of accelerated development, there is a suppression of some of the natural constraints, which prevent divergence. And as the rate of innovation, of discovery and of everything else in the world gets faster and faster so does the *obsolescence of people* and things become ever more acute. The qualitative change that has occurred in the last decade with the development of atomic energy, with the exploration and use of space, with the advent of electronics and computer sciences, is a manifestation of the divergent human function, which has suddenly overtaken the world. What we have witnessed so far, dramatic as it is, is probably pedestrian compared to what we can expect in the future". Sarabhai's prophesy made over 52 years ago has come true with a bang. So let us ask, how is our education system going to prevent the obsolescence of people? Will our education system simply lead to the development of a useless class of people? Should our education system not succeed in providing at least foundational literacy and numeracy to all? Such concerns are also well recognized in the NEP 2020.

Let us ponder over the central issue affecting quality higher education in India. Recruiting worthy faculty is a core issue in universities as reputation of the institution depends on it. In fact, downfall of quality academic pursuits in universities has roots in the faculty recruitment policies and practices. Incompetent and unworthy vice chancellors and faculty have greatly contributed to the deterioration of academic standards. The assessment and accreditation procedures and people involved in it are not above the board either. Often the rankings and grades accorded to varsities differ from the public perceptions. In addition, use of rigid rules in the faculty appointments also has its own repercussions. Such developments cry for recruitment of faculty and varsity leaders based on competency rather than on mere paper qualifications and extraneous factors. In certain domains like the fine arts or performing arts (music, dance, theatre, etc.), yoga, sports to name a few, it is difficult to even to get experts in the form of Professors to conduct interviews for recruitment or promotion of faculty. Use of rigid yardsticks like clearing NET or possessing doctoral degree in the field of performing arts is unproductive. Criteria like these can disqualify even the best and the world-renowned celebrities from serving on the selection committees or for teaching positions in the colleges/varsities. And, this is very embarrassing. Therefore, in all fairness, universities should have freedom to appoint/promote or to invite eminent personalities as professors (and as experts on the selection committees) without insisting on their paper qualifications and affiliation to institutions in fields like the performing arts, sports, and yoga and so on. After all, sensitivity and sensibility should prevail and override rigid, unimaginative, and unrealistic rules. The universities should have autonomy to appoint eminent performing artists as *adjunct* or *visiting professors*, and as *experts* on the selection committees for filling up faculty positions regardless of their paper qualifications.

It is time to find newer and better ways of assessing candidates for recruitment to teaching positions in colleges/varsities that primarily include assessing overall domain knowledge, depth of knowledge in a given field; competency and aptitude for teaching. For higher jobs, performance in the previous jobs and capabilities for the intended jobs (that may require leadership and administrative qualities) should be the criteria for recruitment. Unfortunately, in the recruitment or promotion of faculty, competency is rarely tested before recruiting personnel for intended jobs (teaching, research or administration). Mere paper qualification and number of years of service is considered to be sufficient. As a consequence, on record we have qualified but in reality not so competent faculty at various positions in the hierarchy of higher education institutions (HEIs). Such a scenario can only result in poor quality education as well as undesirable practices, and exploitation of stakeholders. A situation like this is not conducive for transforming universities with rapid growth or quality output. It is relevant to note here that long ago India's first Prime Minister Pundit Jawaharlal Nehru wrote to the State Chief Ministers on June 27, 1961 stating, "I dislike any kind of reservation, more particularly in services. I react strongly against anything, which leads to inefficiency and second-rate standards. I want my country to be a first-class country in everything. The moment we encourage the second-rate, we are lost. The only real way to help the backward group is to give opportunities of good education. But if we go in for reservations on communal and caste basis, we swamp the bright and able people and remain second-rate or third-rate. I am grieved to learn of how far this business of reservation has gone based on communal considerations. It has amazed me to learn that even promotions are based sometimes on communal and caste considerations. In this way lies not only folly, but disaster. Let us help the backward groups by all means but never at the cost of efficiency. How are we going to build our public sector or indeed any sector with second-rate people?" (*Source*: Google). Apparently, it was clear to Nehru that nation cannot be built by compromising competency in the appointment or promotion of personnel working; be it in public or private sector enterprises. Likewise, when recruitment of faculty members based on favouritism, nepotism, corruption and other considerations goes on unabatedly, it will only assure the detriment of the institutions/organizations and the nation. Living examples of such a scenario are seen all over.

The appointments to various key positions like the Vice Chancellors, Registrars, Controller of Examinations (Registrar Evaluation), and membership of the governing bodies like the Executive Council or Syndicate, and Academic Council, disregarding reputation and competency of individuals in question have given lethal blows to many universities. This has led to a downfall of quality of governance and education and rise in unethical practices. In the long run, poor credibility (utility) of credentials (certifications) is sure to pose an existential threat for universities (just as many loss making public sector units); thereby generating scope for mushrooming of private and foreign universities. Unfortunately, such threats are not perceived well, and most HEIs continue their business as usual. It is high time to study and analyse the rise and fall of varsities in India since independence, to enable consolidation of achievements and introspection of failures. It is also time to honestly introspect the consequences of poor funding and faculty recruitment policies. Surely there is an urgent need for policies to ensure national and if possible international footprint of faculty in all universities. Because, only when our higher education system advances to global standards it will be possible to grapple with complex problems arising out of globalization and changing demographic picture of the country.

It is comforting that the future education is poised to undergo drastic changes with a focus on creative thinking, acquiring skills and making innovations. The traditional classrooms and laboratories will need redesigning to facilitate various facets of blended learning and developing skills. The universities need to produce graduates who are not only ready for intended jobs or entrepreneurships but also capable of critical thinking and, ability to apply their knowledge for resolving diverse challenges arising from time to time (even in the same job). Emphasis on skill development is the order of the day. Yet, overemphasis can be harmful. Skills acquired today become obsolete tomorrow; besides it is difficult to predict the nature of future jobs. Therefore, a sound knowledge of core subjects and ability for critical thinking are essential in tackling new as well as diverse problems. Specialization is good but not at the cost of fine grasp of fundamentals. A familiar example pertains to students passing out with post-graduation degree in zoology. In former times, they could be absorbed in schools/colleges and universities to teach zoology, for research in animal sciences, to work as entomologists and pest managers, in hydro-biological, aquaculture and fisheries departments, in dairy forms, departments of parasitology, anatomy, physiology, apiculture, sericulture, aviary and so on. These days, all these positions require specializations. An example in point is the course on 'Sericulture'. Over three decades ago Sericulture was popular and many universities even started a new department to train students in sericulture at PG level. Such departments now stand closed following a shrunken demand for Indian silk which is costlier than the Chinese silk. Consequently, students with master's degree in sericulture are left in the lurch as they can't fit well into other departments unlike the regular zoology graduates. It indicates a need to balance between skill development, specialization and acquiring sound knowledge of fundamentals; the latter will go a long way in enabling learners to think critically and overcome new challenges. Also, the future graduates need to be more job providers than job seekers; lest India's current demographic dividend (large youth population) may become a liability as it transforms into an old population with the passing of years. Therefore, ideally, education is for training the students in *life skills* and/or *livelihood skills* rather than merely help them get access for higher (degree) classes.

Lastly, the process of human resource development, to which the universities are committed, is indeed very complex and only good education can make it easier to accomplish the goal. Therefore, higher education must inspire building character with moral and ethical values, civic sense and citizenry. The universities have an inescapable responsibility and obligation (to the country) to provide a state of the art education to enable meeting local, national as well as global challenges, and hope for the global citizenship. In any case, "education is the passport to the future, for tomorrow belongs to those who prepare for it today" (Malcolm X; *source*: Google).

Chapter 2

Leadership and Governance

Governance and leadership are the 'Yin and the Yang' of successful organisations. If you have leadership without governance you risk tyranny, fraud and personal fiefdoms. If you have governance without leadership you risk atrophy, bureaucracy and indifference.

— Mark Goyder

Ideal functioning of an institution/enterprise/industry depends generally upon the leadership of the head of the organization and on the quality of governance. The two processes are not mutually exclusive; instead, they are complementary to each other. Accordingly, good governance and leadership impact higher education institutions (HEIs) enormously and in turn the very process and fabric of producing needed human resource for the country. Regional, national and international developments and their sustenance solely depend upon building a sound science and technology base, ability to continuously engage in making innovations and remain competitive all the time. At the same time, management of various societal affairs also requires good human resource. These include, food production (agriculture, milk production, fisheries, etc.), management of national resources (the environment, water, forest, mines, etc.), building infrastructure, making economic progresses, making innovations and managing international affairs, healthcare of citizens, maintaining law and order, defence of the country as well as meeting unforeseen national or international challenges arising from time to time. Alongside, there is a need to balance between the *haves* and *have-nots* such that the society remains stable and peaceful. In short, the entire process of management of the societies and the nation requires quality human resource, the production of which is the sole responsibility of the HEIs, in particular, the universities. Therefore, universities have the sole role of delivering quality education in diverse fields: science and technology (e.g. engineering, medicine, and biotechnology etc.), legal education (national and international laws), business and economics, foreign affairs, inculcation of moral and ethical values and citizenry to name a few.

The education system as a whole should always be in a state of dynamic equilibrium so that it can resonate well with the changing social structures, challenges of globalization, industrial revolutions, and job disruptions etc. The new paradigms of education truly are learning to learn, learning to do, learning to live together and learning to be, all of which demand learning, unlearning and relearning. Financial progress of nations now more than ever depends on the ability to think critically, creatively and on making innovations. In simple terms, innovation is generating value for our research and conversion of knowledge into wealth. In this venture, universities have a key role to play. Hence, for realizing these objectives the qualities of leadership, governance and performance of universities have to be of highest order.

With the above concerns in mind, this chapter highlights the importance of 'leadership and governance' and the importance of proper deployment of various personnel in reinforcing the management of universities, and making their existence worthwhile. Because, it is not enough that the bus is full; right person should occupy the right seat. It must also be borne in mind that no one can become leader without doing more than what she/he is paid for as salary and cannot be successful without developing the art of leadership. The universities need people in all positions with high degree of commitment. Because, people with commitment work for fulfilment, which in the process elevates the stature of the organizations. Incentives cannot substitute for a person's commitments and inner urge towards the fulfilments. This applies to all sections of the organization: teachers, supporting staff and administrators.

As in any organization, the universities need leaders in the form of vice chancellors and, good governance that is not only efficient and transparent but also user-friendly. Leaders are needed for advancement and all-round progress of the institution. Leaders are those who have both short-term and long-term vision for the institution. A leader takes all stakeholders into confidence; motivates and involves them for organizational works and decision-making processes. Leadership is an inherent quality that comes with vision, wisdom, concern and commitments of a person to the institution and the nation. She/he sets benchmark and example by her/his own working style. Indeed, leadership is a process and not a position. A vice chancellor of the university is a facilitator and not a ruler. Further, Vice Chancellorship is an opportunity (1) for providing visionary leadership, (2) for ushering academic progresses and progressions, (3) streamlining administration, and above all, to realize one's own potential in placing the university and education programs on a higher pedestal.

It is obvious that mere vision and leadership are not enough for the betterment of the institution. Leadership should accompany ability for good governance. Efficient governance envisages swift approvals and clearance of files; decentralization and delegation of powers to subordinate officials, transparency in decision-making processes through computerization of all facets of governance (academic, administrative and finance), heralding user-friendliness in administration, and ensuring time bound accomplishment of set goals and decisions taken by various executive and academic bodies of the university. In short, the philosophy of governance has to change from what was set by the colonial masters, the foreign rulers, for their convenience. Their administration was chiefly based on mistrust and therefore created huge bureaucracy. But, we have no reason to continue with the colonial ruler's strategy. In free India administration should be based on trust and elimination of bureaucracy, a shift from mistrust to trust. Indeed it is high time, to reimagine the administration based on trust of the subordinate officials with due decentralization of powers with needed checks and balances. Unequivocally, credibility of universities largely depends upon the quality of governance. Therefore, universities need vice chancellors who possess leadership qualities, ability for good governance and fair commitment for enhancing the image of the university.

It is in the knowledge of everyone that private sectors generally perform better than the public sector units. In private sector enterprises, the Chief Executive Officers (CEOs) are employed on the basis of their competency and performance; they are held responsible and accountable to the organization. Further, in private sectors the policy of 'hire and fire' operates unlike in the public sectors, including the education sector. The officials heading the colleges and universities, the Principals and Vice Chancellors respectively, are not comparable to CEOs of the private sector organizations, in terms of pressure to deliver what is expected of them. They lack both freedom and accountability. Consequently, many vice chancellors and principals comfortably complete their term with insignificant performance. Poor leadership and governance only ruin the institutions; universities are no exceptions. Lowering quality of education has appalling and far-reaching consequences; it destroys the nations. Experience has shown that considerations other than the worthiness in the recruitment and promotion processes invariably contribute to decline in the credibility and soundness of any organization including the HEIs (public or private). Unfortunately, even the private (aided or unaided) educational institutions have failed to build brands despite enjoying certain degree of autonomy and freedom, because they often resort to nepotism and favouritism in the recruitment of faculty and supporting staff. Thus, myopic vision, faulty policies and practices have contributed greatly to the downfall of quality of administration, teaching and research. For instance promotions to leadership roles like, head of the department, principal or vice chancellor are also based on years of service rather than on competency and ability for the intended jobs. This has created a situation where the universities and the PG departments are now headed by persons who are neither endowed with qualities needed to provide leadership and good governance nor the ability to inspire the faculty, students and subordinate officials. Consequently, many universities and their vice chancellors figure in the news for wrong reasons rather than for innovative measures and reforms made in the institution to enhance institutional credentials. Likewise, appointment of other officials of the university; the Pro-Vice Chancellor, Registrar, Registrar Evaluation, members of the Executive Council/ Syndicate/Governing Council without due regard to competency or public image of the incumbents has greatly diminished the administrative machinery. Public and media often criticize the bad incumbents (say vice chancellors) for their incompetency, corruption, nepotism, favouritism and numerous irregularities but conveniently spare the other officials involved in their selection and appointment. In all fairness, besides the incumbents, members who sit on the search/selection committees to recommend the names for vice chancellorships, and the appointing authorities should also share the blame. Expectedly, the incumbents who invest their resources (time and energy spent in lobbying, savings or earnings, etc.) to secure positions, will only engage full time in recovering their investments.

Any government that is interested in improving the university education must first ensure that the top is not defective because leakage and breakage start from the top and percolate down unwaveringly following the law of gravity. Worthy heads of the institution by their honesty, integrity and concerns can transform the mind-set of subordinate officials down to the level of class IV employees and motivate them for virtuous performance. Therefore, quality leadership and good governance are the urgent needs to sustain modern education and credibility of HEIs (Saidapur 2019bc). A starting point of ensuring good leadership, governance, management and remodeling of universities is the appointment of worthy vice chancellors and other officials as well as placing eminent persons on the statutory bodies like the Executive Council/Syndicate, Academic Council, Board of Studies (BOS) and selection committees. Ensuring proper faculty recruitment and allowing eminent professors who have vision to head the PG departments and BOS can herald needed academic progresses. The following sections deal with these aspects as well as student support systems and management of extracurricular activities that are equally important.

1. Appointment of Vice Chancellors

The vice chancellors are fully responsible for smooth and efficient management of the universities. The position of vice chancellorship is not about merely controlling or managing administration; it is largely about providing leadership. A vice chancellor should clearly envision the intended plans with a roadmap and strive to accomplish the same in his/her term of office, with a well-defined time-bound frame. It is for this reason, a person with known leadership qualities and good academic and administrative credentials, selected on an all India (if not global) level should head a university as its vice chancellor. Honesty, integrity and leadership qualities are the prime virtues of a good vice chancellor and any one holding such a position must command respect of the academic community and the stakeholders. Charismatic professors with upright credentials will command respect and bring reputation to the chair she/he occupies. Such a person will carry out his/her *raja dharma* and treat friends and foes equally. Corrupt and dishonest individuals command least respect among the teaching fraternity, students, supporting staff and stakeholders. Besides, incompetent and corrupt officials are malleable to political interferences. Incompetency shows up in many forms. For instance, when subordinate officials and members of the staff question vice chancellors on certain decisions taken by them, they retort by saying, 'are you questioning my authority'. The authorities may get away for the moment with such assertions but it is always at the cost of their own image and credibility. A sweeping effect of such encounters is that it makes the faculty members feel demoralized. In consequence, the demoralized faculty fails to give its best to the system. Demoralized soldiers cannot win battles leave alone the wars. Keeping the various concerns (raised above) in mind, the search committee as well as the concerned education departments and finally, the appointing authorities must exercise great care and concern while finalizing the list of probable candidates, and their subsequent appointment as vice chancellors.

Shortlisting of names for the position of vice chancellors is normally done by a panel of experts, who are supposed to be eminent scholars in their own respective fields of studies. The names of experts are suggested as per the provisions of the given University Act. For instance, in the State of Karnataka, members of the search committee are those nominated by the UGC, by the Chancellor of the Universities (Governor of the State), the university Syndicate and the Department of Higher Education (one from each). The expert nominated by the government serves as the Chairperson of the committee. In recent years even sitting vice chancellors (who were candidates themselves a few months ago!) are made members of the search committee. Legalities apart, this is not a good practice despite its handiness to the nominating authority. The sitting vice chancellors of State varsities are subservient to both State government and the Chancellor and as such enjoy little freedom to deviate from the suggestions coming from them. In fact, this is a blatantly bad practice as it brings little credibility to the government, and is avoidable, with no apparent loss to the nominating authority. At the same time, the sitting vice chancellors (at least those who have conscience, courage and conviction) should desist from participating in selecting their own colleagues for sister universities of the same State. Apparently, undisclosed conveniences prevail over principles letting polity rule over the probity. Nonetheless, credibility of actions in the public eye is important for the prevailing governments and therefore, the governments should not give scope for adverse criticisms. The shortlisted names are then submitted to the State Higher Education Department which recommends its choice of name to the Chancellor-Governor of the State. In the case of Central Universities, shortlisting of names is done by the search committees constituted by the Ministry of Education (MOE). Approval of name and appointment of vice chancellors is then done by the President of India. Thus, appointment of vice chancellors turns out to be a political choice.

As the primary responsibility of shortlisting names lies with the search committee it should (1) consist of members with high academic scholarship and integrity, and (2) enjoy total freedom to include names of eminent persons from all over the country or abroad (non-resident Indians). Conditions like working knowledge of regional language may apply where relevant. The

Department of Higher Education should not insist on choosing the names only out of the list of applicants provided and thereby limit the scope of finding worthy persons from national/global pools. Tying the hands of search/selection committee members will do no good for the universities or the States.

Ideally, the governments should evolve proper guidelines for search committees, and provide a list of desirable attributes of candidates to help shortlist names for the position of vice chancellors. Mere academic qualifications are not enough. Administrative acumen and ability to take stakeholders alongwith is necessary. It is but natural that no one provides bad track records in her/his curriculum vitae (e.g. enquires held or pending cases against them for various misdeeds like sexual harassments, mismanagement of funds, dereliction of duties, plagiarism, punishments awarded, etc.). Hence, the person(s) or institutions forwarding the names of prospective candidates should be held responsible for hiding the incriminating facts, misdeeds, strictures passed against the person and enquiries held or pending, if any. Even if a person is exonerated from the accusation, the university should make it clear to the committee. Often exonerations are done for want of evidences and, witnesses turning hostile. Proper checks and balances can help reduce exclusion of undeserving candidates for the top position. A format could be evolved to seek specific information about the prospective candidates to be placed before the search committee. It is in the interest of the State/Federal Governments and the universities to ensure that the prospective candidates for leading the institution have clean record. Mechanisms of transparency will go a long way in building the credentials of the appointing authority, the State/Central Governments as well as the ruling political parties.

In addition to the aforesaid, there should be a clear policy in place that guides shortlisting of candidates for the vice chancellorship. Good standing at the national and international levels, soundtrack records, ability to procure funding from R&D agencies for research and collaborations, administrative experience, ability for working in groups, leadership qualities, and knowledge of University Act, Statutes, Ordinances, Rules and Regulations should be the basis to determine the overall suitability of the candidate for the top position of the universities. Choosing a squint among blind will not help.

In recent times, the universities have been inviting applications for the post of vice chancellor. The very process of *applying* is appalling. It provides enormous scope for lobbying and unethical practices on the part of aspiring candidates. Good academicians lacking political connections and other resources may not even apply for the position. Ideally, the governments in power should invite worthy professors (out of the panel of shortlisted persons by the appropriate committee) to be the vice chancellors as used to be done in former times. Appointment of unworthy, incompetent and corrupt vice chancellors in recent decades has ruined universities and made it almost difficult to reverse the damage. It has in the process made the stakeholders who are at the receiving end helpless. Underserving persons heading the university have great potential to perpetually engage in wrongful practices of serious consequences for the stakeholders and the institution. In such a situation, the main targets are: to be appointed faculty and supporting staff, and developmental works and so on. The faculty and supporting staff in turn exploit students, especially those pursuing research degrees. One gets to hear many horrible stories of exploitation of students by the corrupt supervisors and the ultimate sufferers are not just the students and their parents; the resulting bad human resource is a curse on the nation as corruption spreads quickly across the length and breadth of various institutions.

2. Pro-Vice Chancellor/Rector

Some universities, especially the ones established by the Ministry of Human Resource Development (MHRD) now renamed as Ministry of Education (MOE) have provision to appoint Pro-Vice Chancellors (PVC) or Rectors. However, most State Universities generally do not have such a provision. The position of a rector is quite useful in pursuing specific works assigned by the vice chancellor from time to time. The PVC who is free from the routine administrative hassles can focus on the implementation and monitoring the progression of important programs and processes, within the specified timeframe. A university professor with experience and inclination in administrative matters and acceptable to the vice chancellor can fill the position of the PVC.

3. Registrar, Registrar Evaluation and Finance Officer

In several universities more often than not professors are appointed as the Registrars, Registrar Evaluation (Controller of Examinations) and even as Finance Officers (FO). Unfortunately, many professors are not well conversant with the general 'Rules and Regulations', and 'Service and Conduct Rules'. Hence, appointment of professors for these positions has two major disadvantages: (1) teaching and research are affected and (2) the incumbents find it difficult to take stringent actions on their own colleagues and supporting staff when needed. Furthermore, the NEP 2020 also discourages use of academicians for administrative works. Obviously, it is better to avail the services of bureaucrats from the State/Central Government to fill these positions. The FO has to be a person from finance division of the State or Central governments. All these officials drawn from outside the university system can resolve issues dispassionately by taking decisions as per the prevailing rules. They familiarize themselves with the prevailing 'University Act, Statutes, Ordinances, Rules and Regulations' quickly as they are already familiar with government rules and regulations in general. They can also very easily familiarize themselves with the business rules governing meetings of all statutory bodies of the university. In short, it is desirable that the expertise of Vice Chancellor and the various officials (Registrar, Registrar Evaluation, and Finance Officer) is complementary to each other and not just supplementary in nature. However frequent transfer of such officials will not do much good to the university.

4. Syndicate/Executive Council/Board of Management/Board of Governors

The highest governing body of the university is variously called: Syndicate/Executive Council/Board of Management (BOM)/Board of Governors (BOG), etc., as per the given University Act. The governing bodies need to be such that they exude prestige and social credibility. The members should also possess basic legal acumen and wisdom. Credibility and reputation of governing body members should be such that they command respect from the employees of the university. As these members are considered higher than the varsity professors (in terms of powers and privileges), it is desirable that they are people with high reputation and status in the society. Several members of this body are ex-officio members (being senior professors or Deans or Director of Collegiate Education and so on). A few are nominated by the State Government and the Chancellor/Visitor of the university. It is here that great care needs to be exercised; the nominations made by the State/Central Governments and Chancellors/Visitors reflect their concern and intention. Unfortunately, very unworthy candidates with connections to the power centres often manage to get nominated on such apex bodies of the universities which make the functioning of the governing bodies a mockery. On the other hand, nomination of eminent educationists, social workers, judges, technocrats, and industrialists on such bodies can make a huge difference in the working of the entire university system.

5. Academic Council and Senate

In some universities Academic Council (AC) and Senate are separate bodies while in others the two are combined into Academic Senate. The AC is an important body that makes all academic decisions and policies. Here also, several ex-officio persons, and legislators are made members depending upon the given University Act. In addition, a few members are nominated by the government. Ideally, eminent scholars who may be historians, scientists, legal experts, engineers, educationists and so on drawn from premier institutions and industries should be nominated so that their expertise will enhance academic growth of the institutions and promote vibrant and meaningful deliberations. The nominations should reflect the concerns and betterment of the institution rather the interests of the nominees.

6. Board of Studies

The Board of Studies (BOS) is the most important academic body that is responsible for curriculum development; the various facets of which are described in Chapter 4. The BOS in most universities have a composition with majority of members who are departmental faculty and one or two members from neighbouring varsities. However, such a composition of the BOS is no more useful as it lacks futuristic vision as well as sound knowledge of sub-domains of a given subject. Such a BOS is sure to find it difficult to develop curriculum of global standard depicting modern trends and integration of borderless subject areas in the main subject/paper/course. Challenges and nuances of developing good curriculum are discussed in a later chapter of the book. Evolving new courses with judicious integration of sub-disciplines, borderless areas and courses from other disciplines requires sound domain knowledge and a deeper understanding. Therefore, the BOS should invite eminent faculty members from premier research institutions and industries (serving or superannuated). Various domains of a given subject must be represented by scholars from interdisciplinary areas to facilitate multidisciplinary approach for the study of a given subject. Rigid rules for constitution of BOS are no more useful unless the universities want to do 'business as usual'. Moreover, the universities are now required to evolve 'School' system under which allied or cognate subjects are housed to facilitate multidisciplinary approach in academic processes especially research undertakings. For instance, school of biological sciences may have a single BOS that caters to the needs of plant sciences, animal sciences, microbiology, biotechnology and biochemistry. The school also needs inputs from other science departments (e.g. mathematics, statistics, computer science, and physics) and hence experts from these subject domains should be invited to participate in the BOS meetings whenever curriculums are to be prepared or revised. Likewise, there could be a single BOS for Economics, Commerce and Business Management departments all placed under a school system. Sociology, Social Work and Anthropology departments may also have a common BOS. Similarly, there could be a single BOS under the school of languages for various language courses offered in the institution. These are representative and suggestive examples. Many BOS with the exception of perhaps languages need inputs from mathematical, statistical and computer science experts to strengthen their own subject domains. Therefore, eminent experts can help develop a regionally relevant and globally competent, and outcome-based curriculum in subjects falling under their domain. Lastly, the Chairpersons of BOS should have freedom to invite eminent experts from any part of the country whenever new curriculums are developed.

7. Recruitment of Faculty

Higher education institutions like the universities acquire their fame and reputation primarily because of their faculty and not because of the buildings and infrastructure. Quality education is possible when competent and committed faculty who have concern for the welfare of the students and capable of creating culture of excellence are recruited. Unfortunately, more often than not selection for teaching positions is done based on fulfilment of minimum requirements (possession of required degrees and research publications) rather than on the basis of *competency* and soundness of knowledge in the fundamentals and recent advances in the given subject domain. It is time that we devise methods to assess competency of the candidates for teaching for recruitment to faculty positions rather than get carried away by the publications with their doctoral degree or postdoctoral research supervisors and the impact factors (IF) of journals. Impact factor of the journal has nothing to do with the impact of the work published in a given journal. This awareness has led some countries to ignore IFs while bestowing awards, recognitions or appointing/promoting faculty in the universities. It is beyond doubt that IFs and criteria like the h-index are not necessarily useful in the selection of candidates for various positions, awards and rewards.

Before recruiting or promoting the faculty members, the candidates could be asked to give a colloquium in the concerned departments where students and in-house faculty members interact freely, assess the potential and give their rating on a 0-10 scale and confidential feedbacks. Such a feedback may be considered by the selection committee as an important input on the teaching potential of the candidates. This brings in some amount of transparency in the process of appointments to teaching positions. With the changing scenario of teaching-learning processes, the new teachers need to be conversant with online teaching, use of flipped classrooms, quizzes, group learning, project-based learning, solving solved and unsolved problems. They should be able to promote, learning to think and learning to make innovations in the minds of learners. Therefore, adequacy of candidates in all such parameters must be thoroughly tested before recruitment to faculty positions. Unmistakably, future education is all about creative thinking and making innovations.

As a final point it may be noted that anyone who has no reading habit is unworthy of teaching positions. 'One who does not read has no advantage over one who cannot read', said Mark Twain. Clearly, without books, it is almost impossible to get inspired. Only inspired faculty can inspire students, recommend good books to read and promote reading habit that is fast vanishing. At the same time, the ecosystems of varsities need to improve for good faculty to come. The universities must strive to transform themselves as magnets to attract talents. Vibrant academic environment is more important than small incentives (e.g. extra increments, cash, etc.) in attracting real good talents from all over the country or abroad. There are ample glorious examples of nations before us that have prospered by attracting talent from outside. Highly advanced countries (e.g. USA, Europe, and Australia etc.) have become magnets for attraction of global talents that in a way ensures furtherance of their own progress and prosperity. In a similar vein, India should become magnet of attraction to global talent and thereby facilitate its own growth. In the past, at least some institutions (e.g. Nalanda, Visva Bharati during Tagore era, Aligarh Muslim University and Indian Institute of Science) had some foreign component of faculty. This is totally missing today. Universities should be allowed and cajoled to create adjunct or visiting professorships to facilitate appointment of say five or more eminent persons of Indian or foreign origin for a period of one year at a time, in our universities. This will go a long way in motivating and inspiring the university fraternity as a whole as well as strengthening research activities.

8. Supporting Staff

Evidently, the supporting workers often called as non-teaching staff also need to be competent and committed. They all must have basic knowledge of using computers. In view of the general inadequate number of non-teaching staff some outsourcing has become essential in almost all universities. Outsourcing can be done for certain tasks like: cleaning and maintenance (e.g. electrical and civil works, gardening, binding, printing, hiring vehicles, etc.). Utilizing clerical staff on contract basis is not always a useful way. Computerization and streamlining administration can reduce requirement of manpower. The supporting personnel need short-term orientation and refresher courses periodically for updating with the latest developments in file tracking, maintenance and analysing the data and so on. In India, clerical staff plays a very important and sometimes mischievous role. A case worker, who is usually a junior most clerk (sometimes appointed on compassionate ground or compulsion of promoting even drivers as clerks or appointments made under certain policies of the university/governments, etc.) puts up the file which passes through several tables (e.g. senior clerk, assistant office superintendent, superintendent, assistant registrar, deputy registrar, registrar and then vice chancellor) and all these officials more often than not put their initials habitually. Rarely do they question the case worker or state their opinion. Ordinarily, once the file is cleared by the Registrar, the vice chancellor also puts his signature in a routine way. Most vice chancellors restrain from overruling the opinion of the subordinate officials. To overrule or use the power of discretion, one needs to be thorough in rules and regulations, have convictions and an enlightened mind. Overruling should not be for the purpose of doing injustice or favour. It is an ability to find ways of helping genuinely deserving, meritorious persons in the absence of clear-cut rules or precedence. Reducing delays in the clearance of files and bureaucracy is possible by simple means of decentralizing procedures and proper distribution of works.

9. Digital Library

All university libraries have to undergo metamorphosis in view of the changed scenario. Reading habits have changed.

Ways of accessing literature have changed. Even teaching-learning processes have changed following the introduction of digital online platforms. In short, we need digital libraries with needed infrastructure and other facilities. Therefore, libraries need redesigning to provide service to students, teachers and researchers using modern technologies (see Sathyanarayana, 2019; Joshi, 2019 for more on digital libraries).

10. Support Systems

Student support structures constitute the most important components of any education system. Certain support systems for teachers and supporting staff are also needed. Therefore, each institution may develop its own context and need based support systems. Following are some examples of support systems; given attention they will help improve performance of the institution.

(A) *Student Enrolment*: In universities or their constituent/affiliated colleges, enrolment of students to various courses is the most important activity. The process of admission of students has to be on time, in short time, as per the prevailing norms, and also very transparent. The entire process needs to be digitized. Provision of online admission is very much desirable. In addition, counselling facilities are needed since students apply for multiple courses as they are not sure of securing seats in their desired subject(s) or subject combinations. Some universities have opted for a centralized admission process of students even for their affiliated colleges. Ideally, colleges should be given freedom and regulations to admit students on their own. This can incentivise colleges run by private managements to build brand names and attract good students.

For vitalizing the teaching-learning processes, universities should provide opportunities for cross culture hybridization by making provision for admitting students from different parts of the State, outside the State and a few seats for foreign students where feasible. This will go a long way in making our own students smart; familiarize them with different languages, cultures and food habits of people from different regions. This can also help develop national integration and bring in a kind of national and global perspectives. It is time that both State and the Central Governments think seriously on these lines and evolve appropriate policies to support cross culture hybridization.

(B) *Identity Cards (ID)*: Each student, faculty and supporting staff should be given an institutional photo ID card with a sling. One such card will help avail all facilities on the campus. The photo ID card will help students and employees not only within the institution but also outside the university campus to reveal their bona fide credentials.

(C) *Redesigning Classrooms*: Recent developments in the field of computer science and electronics on one hand and disruptions due to unforeseen pandemics like the Covid-19, deluges, occasional landslides and earth quakes on the other hand have necessitated use of new, mostly online pedagogies in the teaching-learning processes. Furthermore, compulsions of the on-going digital revolution like the *third wave* of internet call for massive changes in the teaching-learning processes and associated pedagogies (see 'Notes' for modern pedagogies). Online teaching has already started even for children studying in kindergarten schools. The new education system is supposed to facilitate training the learners for creative thinking and making innovations. Consequently, the traditional classrooms need to be redesigned and modernized with the state of the art digital technology. Besides, if the 'school' system is adopted, it may necessitate building lecture hall complexes.

(D) *Wi-Fi*: With the boom in information communication technology (ICT) most information is now sought or exchanged predominantly using the internet. The university campuses should become fully Wi-Fi enabled with high-speed connectivity, in the absence of which the online education system will collapse. Even hostels should be well equipped with Wi-Fi facility so that the students can make use of the facilities for their studies, project works and research. The Wi-Fi facility could be made free or subsidized. And, needed precautionary measures to prevent misuse should be in place.

(E) *Dynamic Website*: Every university must have a dynamic website that is updated on day-to-day basis. Website management is a full-time occupation. It should be managed by an expert appointed exclusively for this purpose (the maintenance of which may be outsourced) under the supervision of the officer in charge of 'Internal Quality Assurance Cell' (IQAC). The website should house all necessary data (except the confidential ones); say information related to admission of students in any given year, fee structures, pass percentages, student profiles, student progression, faculty profiles (qualifications, experience, area of specialization, publications, awards and rewards received by them if any etc.), alumni association, scholarships and so on. All pertinent information about academic, co-curricular and extracurricular activities, contact details of the officials of the university, various facilities and provisions (e.g. scholarships, sports or yoga, 'earn while you learn' schemes if any) should be highlighted on the website. The entire prospectus, syllabi of all courses, question papers of the past 5 years may also be placed on the website. The information pertaining to the examinations, meetings, calendar of major events, webinars, and functions and so on may be displayed on the website so as to reduce issuing circulars and use of papers. A dynamic website should have provisions for stakeholder (students, teachers, parents) feedbacks, suggestions and complaints which should be regularly addressed by the concerned authorities.

(F) *Women Related Support Systems*: In the present scenario, number of girl students is roughly equal to the number of boys, and sometimes it exceeds. Therefore, the educational institutions should provide adequate facilities that are routinely required by the girl students. Typically, the building meant for day scholars (ladies) should be cosy and big and in proportion to the number of girl students admitted. It should house a couple of divans for sick and needy, good furniture, lavatories, Wi-Fi, women's magazines, a dining table, water purifier, some indoor games, sanitary napkin vending machine and so on. It is nice to decorate the entire facility with portraits of inspiring women achievers in diverse fields (writers, scientists, social workers, sports personnel, academicians, political leaders and so on). Creating a good ambience for girl students is an essential requirement to promote higher education of girl students as described earlier (Saidapur, 2019c).

(G) *Book Store with Stationery*: Universities may provide space for housing a bookstore and office stationery. Such a store can be run as a cooperative society on a no profit no loss basis with the help of service minded retired faculty or supporting staff and student representatives, in a very transparent manner. The retired employees with passion for social service may be entrusted with the overall management of such stores with the Dean Student's Welfare as the patron. Poor students can have an opportunity to serve in such a store and earn some money (paid on hourly basis or some other criteria). Likewise, a departmental store (mini supermarket) with some permissible countertop medicines can also be set up on the varsity campuses.

(H) *Skill Development, Coaching for SLET/NET and Personality Development*: In addition to catering to the obligatory needs of the prescribed curriculum, it is desirable for the institution to provide opportunity for personality and skill developments, entrepreneurship, and to prepare for various competitive examinations. Such undertakings are best done through outsourcing but not on a commercial mode and, based on the actual demand. In any case, these should be cost effective.

(I) *Special Facilities for the Needy*: It is imperative that all educational institutions have certain model facilities for differently abled persons (in recent times referred as *Divyang or Divyangjan*). For example, ramps for all buildings, elevators for reaching higher floors, special toilets, brail facilities, writers for blind students and so on should be provided. Often institutions claim that they do not have physically challenged students as an excuse for not providing needed facilities. In any case, lack of user-friendly facilities will discourage physically challenged students from enrolling for higher studies. Regardless of whether divyangjan students/faculty members are associated with the institution or not, appropriate facilities should be in place. It is not a question of merely satisfying the statutory requirements or review committees (e.g. NAAC Peer Committee). It is an issue of social concern and empathy towards fellow human beings. Creating needed facilities for *divyang* students reflects sensitivity of the concerned institution towards humanity.

(J) *Endowments, 'Earn while you Learn' Schemes*: Each institute can easily set up endowment lectures, scholarships and book grants with the help of its alumni or other donors. In addition, institutions should think creatively to evolve mechanisms for enabling learners who need to earn some revenue to sustain their studies. Such students could be engaged (e.g. in the library, book store, office, sports section, gardens, guesthouses, canteens, etc.) outside the teaching hours or on holidays and vacation and enable them to earn some revenue.

(K) *Health Centre and Insurance Scheme*: A 'Health Centre' is needed in all universities with facilities for routine lab investigations and dispensing medicine. At the minimum, it should have a qualified permanent or outsourced general physician(s), a nurse and a pharmacist in accordance with the demands of the stakeholders (number of students, faculty and supporting staff). Also, it is desirable to provide insurance cover (health and life) to students of the university towards injuries, illness and accidents. There are different ways of insuring students: either through recognized insurance companies or the institution itself can offer insurance by collecting a nominal sum, say ₹ 100-200 per year from each student enrolled in the university. The latter strategy was adopted in Karnatak University, over a decade ago; it covers hospitalization following unforeseen accidents during the tenure of the students. The scheme covers insurance benefit to students of affiliated and constituent colleges as well. The insurance scheme is working very well. The legal experts can draft the rules pertaining to the operation of insurance funds for approval by the appropriate governing bodies of the university. A good corpus of insurance funds could be created out of the unspent balances each year and enhance support to the insured.

(L) *Sports, National Service Scheme (NSS), Cultural Activities*: Sports, NSS and Cultural and Social Activities constitute important extracurricular activities. A proper management of these activities is therefore important. Assigning management of these activities to faculty members with little or no experience or time will result in poor promotion of these activities. Such assignments also affect teaching and research of the concerned faculty members. Therefore, a simple way out is utilizing services of experts on annual contract basis for a period of 2-3 years with a possibility of renewal for another term following a transparent review and outcome-based performance of the officer in charge. Ideally, services of retired or unemployed experts (State/National level player, superannuated NSS officer, personnel involved in cultural activities) or a social worker available nearby can be utilized for managing extracurricular activities more meaningfully. The offer of such appointments to a prospective expert must be made after a thorough scrutiny, presentation of vision/mission by the incumbent, and interview by a panel of experts to ensure competency, commitment and passion before engaging.

(M) *Yoga*: If a university has Yoga Department, it should be entrusted with the task of enrolling large number of students and employees for yoga classes and promote yoga for good health. Their working need not match with the office hours. The yoga department must be made vibrant and given freedom to have their own time table and working hours. In institutions where no formal experts on yoga are available, outsourcing could be done. Usually, the outsourced personnel perform well and at the same time expenditure will be less.

Most university campuses are used by a large number of morning walkers and joggers. The university could also engage them in the practice of yoga and meditation free of cost or with a nominal fee. This gesture of resonating with the social responsibility will go a long way in keeping the local community healthy and also boosting image of the institution.

(N) *Drinking water and Sanitary Facilities*: Free access to clean drinking water is a basic requirement of all living beings. Hence, the educational institutions must provide adequate facility of clean drinking water at multiple sites on the campus (say at all PG departments, lecture hall complexes, playgrounds, auditoriums and offices). Likewise, clean lavatory facilities for boys and girls should be in multiple places on the campus of the institution.

(O) *Cafeteria:* Good eatery places with basic services are essential. These should be economical and affordable to the students (e.g. self-servicing). The cafeteria should also have separate cubicles or rooms for faculty members and girl students. The cafeterias may be run on self-service mode to reduce expenditures on maintenance and cost of food.

(P) *Guest Houses and Hostels*

(i) *Guest houses*: It is often difficult for universities to maintain high standards of Guesthouse facilities due to various reasons. Yet these facilities need to be well maintained and well managed. Many eminent professors and officials from all over the country and abroad visit universities almost on daily basis and normally stay in the university guesthouses. Consequently, the visiting faculty or other visitors invariably carry impressions about the university governance, based on the experience of their stay in the guesthouse (cleanliness, food quality, service). Therefore, university guesthouses should be run rather in a professional way. They need not be like the 5-star hotels but should be decent enough like a hermitage with clean linen, basic amenities, well lighted and ventilated, providing quality vegetarian food and service, and good ambience.

The university authorities once in a way should make surprise visits and if possible stay overnight in different rooms each time (not just VIP rooms) and experience the comfort and shortcomings and take necessary steps. They can also interact casually over the breakfast with the other residents to know their experiences, and feedbacks. Where necessary, universities may avail the services of professionals for proper management of guesthouses through suitable memorandum of understanding (MOU).

(ii) *Hostels*: Management of students' hostels is often very tricky. Always there will be complaints, particularly about the food quality, water supply or electricity failures, reading room or indoor games and certain other facilities and so on. More often than not, the presence of many non-bona fide persons invariably creates problems to other residents and wardens who are often members of the faculty. The practice of appointing varsity teachers as the wardens needs to be discontinued. The NEP 2020 also recommends and rightly so, that teachers be freed from non-academic assignments. Ideally, the hostel wardens could be outsourced. Terms of reference for outsourcing can be worked out by each institution.

An out of box idea is to consider a new model. Entrust the management of hostels and guesthouses to the postgraduate department of 'Business Management' in case the university has such a department. The teachers and a few students of each batch can use this opportunity for their project work and hands-on experience in the management. At the same time, such a practice may be very useful to the university in evolving newer ways of effectively running the guesthouses/hostels based on the ground level (hands-on) experience. However, suggested structures of management need discussion and approval in the executive bodies of the institution, drafting appropriate guidelines and evolving *modus operandi* to manage them.

Importantly, institution must ensure that guest houses and hostels do not become dens of unauthorized occupation and untoward activities. Furthermore, both Guesthouses and Hostels should earn some revenue to the university and the earnings should be set aside separately and utilized to meet the recurring expenditures, annual maintenance and renovation works of these facilities.

(Q) *Mentoring and Counselling Cells*: In this modern, highly competitive world with severe competitions of all kinds, students are often subjected to stress and strain. Ability to withstand the stress is not uniformly same among all boys and girls. The distressed young students need timely counselling. Otherwise it can result in unpleasant and sometimes irreversible consequences. Evidently, timely counselling and mentoring play a very constructive role in the life of students. Ghosh (2019ab) has recently deliberated on the importance and need for mentoring and counselling the students; she also provides simple ideas on how teachers can also be involved in mentoring and counselling activities with little training. However, universities may also have professional counsellors.

(R) *Overall Maintenance Activities*: All universities, as a rule have annual maintenance requirements with respect to various scientific equipment(s), hostels, computers, gardens, cleaning buildings and other facilities like electrical fittings, water supply, plumbing and so on. It is better to outsource maintenance of these facilities by evolving appropriate mechanisms. Such outsourcings will be generally economical and bring in accountability as well as better outcome. The universities when freed from such mundane issues they can concentrate on more vital issues and strive to accomplish their perceived goals. Good support systems are sure to enhance enrolment of students to higher education especially those of the girl students. Each institution must strive to create its own academic and social ecosystem that is congenial in enhancing curricular, extracurricular and cultural activities and sports.

(S) *Parent-Teachers Association*: Generally, colleges have parent-teacher associations but not the universities. There is no harm if the universities or their various postgraduate departments or centres form such associations for exchange of ideas, information and review of career prospects of students. This will help the institution to get useful feedback, reflections on the courses/curriculums. In addition, institutions can gain confidence of the parents.

11. Planning and Monitoring Board

All universities need a 'Planning and Monitoring Board' (PMB) consisting of experts from various domains like, academic, administrative, legal, social work, industry, sports and so on along with Deans of various faculties, one EC/Syndicate/Governing body member and university officials like the Registrar, Controller of Examinations and Finance Officer. An eminent academician with a good track record should chair the committee. Hence, the Chairperson should be higher in the stature compared to the sitting vice chancellor. The serving vice chancellor may act as a Co-Chairperson and Convener. The terms of reference relating to PMB (composition, frequency of meetings, expected tasks, inviting experts, preparing road maps, etc.) should be explicit to enable smooth functioning. The recommendations of the PMB should guide the university in its progressive march. The PMB should ensure continuity of progress in accomplishing the evolved road maps; for this to happen it is desirable that the term of office of the Chairman, PMB overlaps at least for a year between the terms of two successive vice chancellors.

12. Decentralization of Powers

In organizations like the university, governance is the most crucial determinant upon which depends efficient and orderly functioning of the institution in all spheres: academic, administrative, finance, examination division and extracurricular undertakings. Efficiency, transparency and swiftness in overall administration help establish credibility in the minds of stakeholders. A centralized power structure and decision-making often result in delays in taking decisions, clearance of files, execution of decisions taken in the various statutory bodies, and diminish overall efficiency. On the other hand, a larger participation of the administrative machinery speeds up decision-making processes and clearance of files, and bring in transparency in the administrative processes, and stakeholder satisfaction. Moreover, 'accountability' and 'freedom' go hand in hand and as such responsibility of good governance must be shared by all connected with the organization. Without first giving freedom to subordinate officials, they cannot be held seriously accountable for their performances. For a successful management of the institution all stakeholders must be taken into confidence. Sharing responsibility by all in the organization will invariably enhance general administration. Therefore, the universities should also decentralize and delegate powers to their subordinate officials. It is noteworthy that Karnatak University, decentralized the administrative processes long ago in the year

2007 through delegation of administrative and financial powers to various officials (see Appendix-1 for details). Such delegation of powers helps in reducing the mundane works of the vice chancellor and generates more time to chalk out visionary plans for a futuristic development of a university. At the same time, it increases efficiency and accountability of all officials, reduces bureaucracy and brings in transparency in administration. In the process, the stakeholders are benefitted. After all, good governance is all about efficient management of the institution.

13. Enlightened Leadership

As far as the enlightened and effective leadership of vice chancellors is concerned, few names come to the mind. These are Sir Ashutosh Mukherjee, Madan Mohan Malaviya, Sir S. Radhakrishnan, and a few more. However, no one can ever match the vision and courage of conviction with Sir Ashutosh who was an eminent academic, educationist and a jurist. It is he who discovered C.V. Raman and S. Radhakrishnan. Indian universities need leaders like him. Sir Ashutosh was the second Indian vice chancellor of Calcutta University and held the position for a record five terms (1906-14 and 1921-23). He was a man of high academic integrity, self-esteem and immense national pride. He was known for recognizing young talents. In 1917, Sir Ashutosh wanted to strengthen physics education in the newly started university college. Of all the people, he spotted C.V. Raman a person working for Government of India as the accounts officer and doing research at the 'Indian Association for the Cultivation of Science' (IACS), Calcutta (now Kolkata) in his free time outside the office hours. Sir Ashutosh wrote to Government of India for sparing services of C.V. Raman to work in Calcutta University for two years as an 'experimental' professor of physics. The Viceroy's Council however did not permit. Not deterred by this, Sir Ashutosh offered Raman the newly created Taraknath Palit Professor of Physics Chair for which he was not qualified as per the conditions stipulated i.e. having not received any higher training abroad. Secondly, the emoluments were far lower than what Raman was already getting in the government service. Interestingly, Raman accepted the Palit Chair despite small salary. Rest is history. Raman earned the distinction of being the first Asian to bag the Noble Prize in science (1930). Sir Ashutosh was also responsible to cajole the young philosopher Sarvepalli Radhakrishnan (then working in Mysore University) to occupy Philosophy Chair at Calcutta University who later became the President of India and whose birthday is celebrated as 'teachers' day. Sir Ashutosh took several such decisions against the odds, inspired by his own courage of conviction, and for promotion of education. Sir Ashutosh declined to be reappointed to a 6th term as vice chancellorship of Calcutta University in 1923 when the Chancellor of the University and Governor of Bengal the Earl of Lytton, tried to impose certain conditions on his reappointment. Shortly hereafter, he also resigned his judgeship on Calcutta High Court. He was rightly called the "Tiger of Bengal". Where are such vice chancellors with courage of conviction and respect for scholarship, the likes of Sir Ashutosh Mukherjee in the present times?

Another worthy example pertains to the award of a research scholarship to the mathematical genius Srinivasa Ramanujan by the Madras University despite his not having even a graduation degree. In a historic session (on April 7, 1913) Syndicate of Madras University passed a resolution, at the recommendation of BOS in Mathematics, to sanction research scholarship of ₹ 75 per month to Srinivasa Ramanujan a young prodigy who was striking a new path in mathematics, for a period of two years. The decision was not easy as such scholarships are given to PG degree holders. How could the University of Madras bend the rules and grant scholarship to Ramanujan? It is said, that following disagreements in the governing body meeting the then vice chancellor Shri P.R. Sundaram Iyer, also the Chief Justice of Madras High Court, rose and asked members: "Did not the preamble of the Act establishing the University specify that one of its functions was to promote research? And whatever the lapses Ramanujan's education was he not a proven mathematical researcher?" The argument won the day. Authorities stretched the rules to accommodate Ramanujan. The Registrar of the university obtained express consent of the Governor of Fort St. George in Council. Within a week, by April 12, Ramanujan received the good news. This is a best example of how bodies like BOS and

Syndicate with enlightened leadership given by vice chancellor and support from the efficient Registrar can make a difference. Thanks to such enlightened leadership of the then vice chancellor (Shri Sundaram Iyer) and support of all officials of that time, the bust of Ramanujan now stands adoring the Cambridge University, UK to an eternal pride of India. It is very apt to recall the quote of Peter Drucker who said, "Effective leadership is not about making speeches or being liked; leadership is defined by results not attributes". The two examples of enlightened leadership of the yester year vice chancellors should suffice to inspire the contemporary counterparts of the current century. Also, the examples serve to underscore that at times, leadership requires bending rules though without breaking them, for overall good of the institution and deserving persons.

Lastly, the two major roles of vice chancellors are: (1) providing good governance, and (2) giving academic leadership. However, mere governance without leadership is futile. And leadership without good governance is also futile. Therefore, leadership and governance must go hand in hand. Further, a vice chancellor should be more like a philosopher king, a visionary and one who strives for long-term welfare of the stakeholders—the students, faculty and the Society at large. The Vice chancellors are merely the facilitators and guardians of higher education and research. They are not the rulers of the universities. Finally, enlightened leadership and ability for good governance of the head of the university matter a lot in establishing credibility and confidence in the minds of stakeholders and general public. Today, more than ever, the universities need to build credentials by ensuring the utility value of various certificates, diplomas and degrees they award. Indeed, this is the biggest challenge of universities and the governments in power; especially in the twenty-first century context which is highly complex, competitive and fast changing in its dynamics worldwide.

To conclude, good governance is like an orchestra where everyone must play diligently to produce melody. The universities run well with the combined efforts of the Vice Chancellor, Registrar, Registrar Evaluation, the Finance Officer and the various executive bodies, faculty and supporting staff. Therefore, for success of the universities the various positions must be held by competent people with commitment. Unfortunately, political and other considerations in appointing the officials and nominating incompetent members on the executive bodies have greatly diminished the quality of administration to a level that is alarming and harming. Mediocre persons holding important positions will only bring mediocrity. Like begets like; it is a nature's rule. Logically, smooth and efficient running of universities depends largely on the performance of various personnel serving on key positions. This necessitates placing right person in right place. It is not enough if the bus is full; all seats must be occupied by right persons.

Chapter 3

Management of Fiscal Resources

A judicious management of finances is a basic requirement for development and sound health of the University.

A crucial aspect of the university is its financial soundness that is principally determined by proper management. Generally, finance management of the university is left to the Finance Officer (FO) who looks after the routine transactional affairs. Most vice chancellors do not closely associate themselves in the finance management partly because of the work pressure related to general administration and, poor background knowledge of fiscal management. A sound knowledge of financial management is important because it helps in avoiding and overcoming fiscal deficits and thereby improves the financial health of the institution to a great extent. Involvement of vice chancellors in the management of finances also provides good insight on financial matters of the university and reduces habitual dependence on the generally uninspiring finance officials. Learning about the fiscal matters can help in averting unwarranted problems. Besides, ensuring financial soundness is a key factor in the development of universities. This chapter is based on the author's experiences and insights gained in the process of streamlining and reorganizing receipts and expenditures and overall management of university finances. Hopefully, such insights will also be useful in the management of fiscal resources and bettering the financial status of other universities in the country. Further, the ideas and experiences presented in this chapter may help add some more rewarding dimensions to otherwise dull and boring aspect of administration like the fiscal management of the university, especially for an academic minded vice chancellors and professors involved in the process.

It is well-known that management of university finances is often not taken very seriously by most well-meaning vice chancellors, and the officials serving on deputation from the government as they hold their positions for a short term of 2-3 years depending upon the rules of the State/Central Governments. For reasons of convenience, generally a FO deputed from the government service for specified terms manages the university finances. When the concerned government departments fail to depute their personnel, the post of FO is often held by some professor of the university. In any case, the FO as a rule, attempts to conserve funds, ensure utilization of funds as per prevailing finance codes and runs the accounts section mechanically in a routine manner. The FO is not necessarily a visionary. Often she/he does not look beyond the fiscal year. Typically, accounts personnel are neither very farsighted nor concerned about the long-term welfare of the institution. Their business is to monotonously resolve day to day issues. Even the finance committees evince little interest in planning and preparing annual budgets. However, a carefully made annual budget plan not only shows the current choices made but also reflects on how it is likely to affect the future of the institution. Therefore, vice chancellors with vision, concern and commitment for the university have to involve themselves and provide leadership in preparing the annual budgets as well as for improvement of the financial soundness with innovative ideas. A boring work can thus be converted into a meaningful as well as delightful venture.

Financial crunch is a common phenomenon of the State Universities. The Central Universities that are set up by the union government suffer little from any dearth of funds. Typically, the State Universities depend on the student fee, affiliation fee, interest earned on the deposits and examination fee which is just enough to manage the expenditures. But, often such income is grossly inadequate for undertaking new initiatives, developmental activities, repair and maintenance of old buildings and so on. A meagre income prevents universities from undertaking essential or futuristic developmental works or support research programs of the young faculty by way of seed money. In view of such constraints, judicious management of available funds, the 'receipts and expenditures' is inevitable and it is certain to play a vital role in the smooth running of especially the State universities. Poor management of fiscal resources will only intensify the existing woes.

The State universities receive funds from the respective State governments, principally towards the salary of employees, teaching and supporting staff. For most other expenditures, universities depend upon their own sources of income mentioned above. Hence, received revenues need to be properly managed. This Chapter describes some simple measures that can go a long way in a prudent management of varsity finances. It is worth noting that reorganizing financial management enabled Karnatak University to create substantial amount of corpus (over Rupees Four Crores), during the first year of the author's term in office (ref: No. KU/FOS/4559 dated 13.8.2007 from the Finance Section of the university).

Most State universities cater to good number of affiliated colleges running in their jurisdiction. The NEP 2020 advocates discontinuation of affiliation system over a span of about 15 years or so. However, 15 years is a long time and whether this will ever happen is uncertain. In the meantime, fee collection from different sources and their remittances to the university need vigilant management. The universities generally have constituent colleges and postgraduate (PG) centres in different cities in addition to their own PG departments in the main campus. In addition, some universities have provision for 'external students' who enrol to various courses in Arts, Humanities and Social Sciences and even Science courses (in some varsities). Some universities offer UG/PG courses on 'Distance Education' mode. Thus, the state universities that cater to large population of students must have a rational finance management system for handling huge numbers of receipts and expenditures (e.g. fees pertaining to students' admission, examination, issue of certificates and marks cards, certification of transcripts, and so on). Following are some specific examples of rationalizing income and expenditures in a typical affiliating university.

1. Student Fee Receipts

The various provisions related to receipt and expenditures substantially increase record and account keeping works as the universities receive large number of cheques and demand drafts (DDs) submitted by students and institutions (affiliated and constituent colleges). Therefore, great care is needed in properly documenting such receipts and ensuring their submission to the bank, lest the bank drafts get expired. The whole process from receipt of cheques and DDs to their reconciliation needs to be streamlined and properly regulated. Ideally, cheques and DDs must be encashed within 2 weeks after they are received. Uncaring case workers often allow lapse of cheques/DDs without bringing it to the notice of higher authorities. If this is unchecked, it may even become a habit. This can eventually result in great financial loss to the institution. It is important to note that cash flow for day-to-day expenditures of the university depends largely on various fee receipts. Therefore, a stringent management of fee receipts is very much warranted. In recent times, funds are transferred from colleges to the university online and this has to an extent reduced the manual labour of accounts staff.

A small portion of fee given by the students at the time of enrolment in the affiliated colleges is remitted to the university under many heads like, admission, registration, sports development, college development, gymkhana, NSS, poor students aid fund, youth festival, students welfare fund, career guidance, insurance and so on to name a few. Different universities have different systems of receiving their share from the affiliated colleges. The general practice has been that each college sends one demand draft (DD) for each item (say NSS) to the university after completion of the admission process. Therefore, on an average a college will send 8-10 or even more DDs at different points of time, after the completion of the admission process. For a hypothetical calculation, we may presume that an affiliated college sends 10 DDs (one for each item like NSS, etc.) after completion of the student enrolment process. Next, let us presume that a university 'X', on an average caters to 300 affiliated colleges (some universities have 500-1000 colleges). This means handling 300 × 10 = 3000 DDs by the university on account of student admission in affiliated colleges. Bulk of the work it involves is mind boggling: receiving 3000 envelopes in the inward section of the university, their entry in the register book, sending them to the Registrar and then from there to the Finance Officer (FO) who will get them again recorded in the inward register of his/her office and then send them to respective case workers/sections and from there to the bank for encashment. All this means, use of so much stationery and postage (for colleges), making numerous entries, and too much work for the university/finance section and the banks! Consequently, the task of mere handling DDs requires considerable man power. Is there a way out? Yes. All a university can do is to prepare a 'Table' with columns and rows to list various heads serially, against which, number of students admitted, prescribed fees on each head of account, fee collected, can be listed. Total fees collected by a college under each head can be depicted in the last column. Finally, Grand total of fees collected by the colleges under various heads (share of the university) can be easily computed. Such a table giving all needed information can then be sent to the university along with a single DD; in one stroke 3000 DDs get reduced to 300 (one per college) and reduction in the quantum of work to 1/10th for personnel involved in the procurement of DDs, dispatch sections, making entries in the inward registry at the university/Accounts section, and overall work of the banks and so on. In essence, this also helps in significant saving of stationary, postage, and in the avoidance of unproductive labour. More, importantly, such an exercise promotes efficient management of funds with less manpower.

2. Endowments, Gold Medals and Scholarship Deposits

In any university there will be several endowment funds (that remain permanently with the institution) pertaining to the award of gold medals, prizes and scholarships. There will be hundreds of such deposits. Interest amount on these is utilized for the purpose for which the endowments are made. There is no need to maintain large number of term deposit receipts and increase the work of handling these (renewals and maintenance). Instead, merging the large number of deposits into a few receipts (e.g. pooling all receipts pertaining to gold medal as one receipt and so on) will reduce quantum of works related to management of such deposits and enhance the ease of handling, renewals, maintenance and so on.

3. Management of Affiliation Deposits

The affiliated colleges deposit certain specified amount in the university. Such deposits are refundable if and when the college is closed permanently or disaffiliated (processes that are rarely encountered). Customarily, universities deposit such funds in banks for a fixed term (a year or more) and earn some interest amount. Such deposits are renewed as and when they mature. The interest so earned may or may not be given to the concerned college depending upon the agreement between the colleges and the university. In any case, the affiliating universities have to maintain large number of such deposits which mature on different dates. So the finance section has to keep track of such deposits round the year and get them renewed on their maturation. This is cumbersome but avoidable using a simple method. The finance section can easily prepare a consolidated list of such deposits and make a single term deposit in the bank. Renewing a few deposits (various accounts) for additional terms is a least cumbersome process. In short, seemingly simple, restructuring and reforms in the finance section help in (1) rationalizing the receipts and expenditures, (2) reducing the requirement of manpower, (3) increasing the efficiency of finance office works, and (4) ensuring smooth flow of cash for day-to-day works. To illustrate the benefits of such an exercise at Karnatak University the finance section could shrink the number of fixed deposit receipts pertaining to affiliation of colleges from 675 to just 11. Renewing small number of term deposits is simple and less cumbersome to the university as well as to the banks. During such an exercise, interestingly, the university discovered that several colleges had not paid the affiliation deposits for years!

4. Receipts from Examination Wing

The examination wing receives large number of cheques and DDs each day towards some or the other services like verification of marks, revaluation of answer papers, and issue of duplicate marks cards, certificates, examination related aspects and convocation fee and so on. These need to be reconciled as soon as possible so that there is a cash flow for day-to-day requirements. The reconciliation of cheques and drafts is done by the FO. Unfortunately, often there is considerable delay in forwarding cheques and drafts from the examination wing to the university finance section and sometimes the validity of these expires due to delays. Consequently, often the expired cheques and drafts are simply destroyed by the lower staff, out of fear of disciplinary action for allowing them to expire. In addition, there can be at times malpractices and the drafts are reused for another student and so on. Such practices are very harmful to the financial health of the university. Therefore, the Registrar Evaluation (Controller of Examinations) should have a system of sending the cheques and drafts for encashment to finance section as soon as possible, say at the least within 15 days with needed details about the cheque/draft (e.g. date on which it was received, the purpose, amount, etc.). Streamlining management of receipts and expenditures pertaining to the examination wing of the university is thus very crucial in ensuring cash flow for day-to-day requirements. At the same time, prevention of leakages is very important. Recall what Benjamin Franklin once stated. He said, "beware of little expenses: a small leak can sink a great ship". This is applicable to all organizations including the universities.

5. Facilitating Smooth Utilization of Funds of R&D Grants

As a rule, the universities run by the State governments receive grants to meet expenditures on salary of the employees and very little for development and research. Almost all research funding usually comes from different Research & Development (R&D) agencies like University Grants Commission (UGC), Council of Scientific and Industrial Research (CSIR), Department of Science and Technology (DST), Department of Biotechnology (DBT), Indian Council of Agricultural Research (ICAR), Indian Council of Medical Research (ICMR), Department of Environment (DOE) and so on. It is therefore very important that the researchers are facilitated to fully utilize the sanctioned amount without much hurdle and cumbersome processes. And, this is possible if the university authorities that include, Vice

Chancellor, Registrar, Planning and Development Officer and the FO, take proactive measures to facilitate smooth operation of research projects and utilization of funds. Obviously, it calls for a perfect coordination between the Planning & Development Officer, various other university authorities and chairpersons of PG departments. Universities should never allow research funds to lapse. Allowing the sanctioned funds to lapse, only to eventually return the unspent balance to funding agencies is an unaffordable luxury, and a bad remark on the institution. Going a step ahead, universities may even have a mechanism to penalize those responsible for lapse of funds. At the same time, in order to facilitate smooth and hassle-free utilization of funds the procedures involved should be as user-friendly as possible. Often researchers feel that getting funds for research is easy but their utilization is difficult due to too many bureaucratic norms of the institution. Universities need to be caring to the investigators who bring money, conduct research, guide doctoral students, publish research papers, and bring name to the university as well as build assets for the institution. Further, the institutions should proactively encourage teachers to secure funds for their research and also hold such faculty members in good esteem. A great step in this direction is evolving user-friendly guidelines for operation of funds. Universities with the help of distinguished academicians, Registrar and FO may prepare 'User-Friendly Guidelines for Operation of R&D Grants' (see Appendix-3) and procure approval of the apex bodies of the institution (Syndicate/EC/BOM/BOG). Simplifying procedures for utilization of funds will encourage faculty members to write research proposals and secure grants and enrich the universities and promote quality academic pursuits.

Equally important to providing user-friendly guidelines for use of research grants, is timely auditing and issuing utilization certificates without harassing the investigators. Authorities should ensure that the auditors do not unduly trouble the investigators. Universities could identify a few Chartered Accountants and outsource the auditing processes of funds secured under R&D agencies for speedy issue of 'Utilization Certificates'. It will promote timely release of further instalments, and procurement of additional grants. It is the vice chancellors who should convince the auditors about the importance of procuring R&D funds and to restrain from making unnecessary audit observations; this will go a long way in building infrastructure, labs and research facilities as well as building brand name to the university. An upright vice chancellor has nothing to fear from the auditors or their objections.

Finally, there exists an interesting phenomenon in most universities/institutions pertaining to unutilized funds of R&D agencies (especially UGC). Often the unutilized funds are not returned in time and remains with the university. The tragedy is neither the UGC is in a position to monitor the quantum of such refunds that are due from various universities, nor the institutions holding such amount are in a position to spend it. Therefore, it is a good idea to pool such unspent balances and keep it as fixed deposits in the banks. It is still better if the UGC issues a circular allowing the institutions to spend the unspent balance in an appropriate way; say for strengthening university's 'Central Instrumentation' facilities and so on. The relevant files can then be formally closed.

6. Student's Insurance

Students of affiliated, constituent colleges and PG departments need some kind of insurance to cover hospitalization expenditures following unforeseen accidents and deaths during their study period. Either one can opt for providing insurance protection using established insurance companies or the university can have its own insurance plan carefully drawn with the help of legal experts. This can be both student-friendly and less expensive at the same time. As an example, Karnatak University developed such a scheme around the year 2007 with meagre contribution from each student. It gave cover to all bona fide students of the university towards hospitalization, accidents, etc. Further, all amount collected may not get exhausted in a given financial year. Therefore, unspent balance could be used to build *'Insurance Corpus Fund'*. Depending upon the quantum of corpus funds, insurance coverage can be enhanced without burdening the institution. This can be done even with respect to the university employees.

7. Book Store with Stationery

Universities should have outlets for sale of books, stationery and computer accessories etc. The superannuated supporting staff/teachers may run the store on a registered cooperative society basis with minimal profits to cover certain recurring expenditures so that students, teachers and other employees are benefitted. In addition to books and notebooks, office stationery, uniforms and such other items like coffee mugs with university logo, cravats and scarfs with university logo, table calendars and so on can also be made available to the buyers. The entire sale-purchase and accounting should be properly structured and remain transparent with a service motto to help the students and create a kind of win-win situation for both the bookstore and the stake holders. Even if this generates only a small amount after meeting the maintenance expenditures, it is worth the trouble and can gain confidence and appreciation of stakeholders. Needy students can be employed on hourly honorarium basis to serve in such stores under the 'Earn while you Learn' schemes of the university outside the teaching hours or on holidays/vacations.

8. Harnessing the Potential of Alumni

All teaching institutions from primary school to university should have their Alumni Associations (AA) that are registered under 'Society's Act' and headed by a prominent Alumnus who has time and passion to contribute for an all-round development of her/his alma mater. Unfortunately, most colleges and universities have no registered AA; if they have one it is often defunct. Undoubtedly, the former students (Alumni) can play a very useful role in strengthening the institutional activities in variety of ways. Seemingly, with the exception of a few other premier institutions (e.g. IITs, IISc) the real potential of AA is not harnessed well.

As far as the universities are concerned, each year, thousands of students pass out of the institution. Every student of the affiliated/constituent colleges is also an alumnus of the affiliating university. For that matter recipients of honorary doctorate degrees are also alumni of the university and their names may adore the AA. Alumni are indeed very important because it is they who hold their institutions in greatest esteem; who else can surpass them in this regard? Besides, several alumni would have occupied key positions in the society in India or abroad. Most non-resident Indians would be too happy to donate funds generously for instituting scholarships and endowment lectures in the name of their loved ones back in India. The non-resident Indians staying abroad may also support modernizing infrastructure. However, a dynamic website of AA and transparency in the utilization of funds received, is essential to establish credibility of the organization. Every alumnus will be too happy to get involved in the affairs of the institution and also contribute her/his might. AA is a goldmine. Moreover, with time, support for educational institutions by the State or federal governments is more and more likely to wean rather than become generous. Hence, harvesting the potential for AA will go a long way in building universities. But, universities have to have credible, simple and efficient mechanisms to enrol students as members of the AA and visibly promote their activities. The institution should extend full cooperation to AA. The AAs should enjoy full freedom and no interference from the host institution. At the same time, caution is needed to ensure the AA/universities do not breach the trust between them and the donors. For instance, donors would have generously donated funds for institution of annual endowment lectures in the name of some eminent person. If such lectures are not held by the AA/ institution, it amounts to breach of trust between the donors and the institutions; the latter become legally liable for punishment. Establishing and nourishing AAs and harnessing their potentials are described recently (Shanbhag, 2019b).

9. Utilization of Unused Campus Spaces for Generating Funds

Most universities with the exception of those in metropolitan cities have large sized campuses (~500-1000 Acres). Hence, there remains considerable space that is unutilized. Indeed, freely available spaces (say 100-400 acres) can be fruitfully utilized to grow plants of horticulture and floriculture interest or that needed for a paper industry and so on using a—Public-Private

Partnership (PPP) model. Depending upon what is grown, harvesting the yield may begin between 1-3 years, and the university will then start earning significant amount (dividend) annually thereafter. However, some precautions need to be taken. The so-called environmentalists often object for growing plants like the eucalyptus under the pretext that these draw more ground water. This problem can be overcome with proper rain-water harvesting system in place and avoiding pure monoculture plantation. If fruit yielding plants like papaya or grapes or pomegranates are grown then there is no serious problem. Similarly, it is possible to rent classrooms and auditoriums for running evening classes and for academic functions of private organizations and thereby generate some funds. However, proper administrative mechanisms (e.g. fixing rent and other issues) and rules governing the same have to be in place.

10. Creation of Corpus Funds

Importance of corpus funds hardly needs emphasis. Sooner or later every university must create substantial amount as corpus fund. Ideally, it should be at least to the tune of 100 Crore rupees so as to yield decent sum in the form of annual interest amount; it can facilitate sustenance of overall campus development without having to solicit funds from funding agencies or State Governments. The corpus funds should never be used under any circumstances. Only the interest earned and accrued is to be used. The unspent balance at the end of each fiscal year must be added to the corpus and allow its own growth over the years. Further, it is a good idea for the State Governments to contribute matching funds to the university towards the build-up of corpus each year. Even if the State Governments contribute say one or two Crores annually towards the corpus fund of the university it will go a long way in building huge corpus. The dividends from the corpus funds come handy for repair and maintenance as well as for other creative activities.

11. Rastriya Uchchatar Shiksha Abhiyan (RUSA) Scheme

Declining educational standards in the recent decades, poor or obsolete infrastructure, crunches in funds and faculty, large increase in the number of eligible youths seeking higher education are too well known. On realizing the need to upgrade infrastructure and faculty development (competency and skills) in response to globalization and the resulting competitions, the Ministry Human Research Development (MHRD; recently renamed as Ministry of Education) established *Rastriya Uchchatar Shiksha Abhiyan* (National Higher Education Mission) popularly known as RUSA in the year 2013. It aims at supporting colleges and universities recognized by UGC under its Act [clause 12B and 2(f)] as well as those that do not fall under these criteria of eligibility. The scheme is to usher good governance for bringing in academic, administrative, and financial reforms and attain autonomy, freedom, flexibility, as well as accountability at the level of both States and the institutions. RUSA is a well thought out scheme of central funding for State Higher Education. It has defined guidelines for the constitution of various governing bodies and structures at various levels. In brief, RUSA is a scheme for planned expansion of access, equity and excellence in higher education. The ratio of Central and State funding varies depending upon the institution; 90:10 for North-Eastern States, 65:35 for other States and Union Territories; 50:50 for private aided institutions. The funds are given for both infrastructure and quality improvement. Institutional perspective plans, commitments of the State and the recipient institutions are key elements to attract RUSA funding. The State Higher Education Council (SHEC) has a major role in bringing in reforms not only in its structure and functioning but also for the entire State machinery. As per RUSA norms, SHEC is "an autonomous body that will function at an arm's length from the State Government". Apparently, this requires considerable will on the part of the State Governments. Not all States have their SHECs in place. Even if they have one it is often not structured as per the spirit of RUSA norms. The higher education councils are invariably headed by the Education Ministers; however, ideally RUSA programs should be managed by eminent academicians of national and international standing.

The institutions interested in procuring grants from RUSA must obtain current details from their respective SHECs or from its website before applying for funds. The RUSA components broadly include:

1. Setting up new universities
2. Upgradation of autonomous colleges to universities
3. Conversion of colleges to cluster universities
4. New model colleges
5. Upgradation of degree college to model colleges
6. Infrastructure grants to universities
7. New professional colleges
8. Infrastructure grants to colleges
9. Research, innovation and quality improvement
10. Equity initiatives
11. Faculty recruitment support
12. Faculty improvements
13. Setting up Research Universities
14. Vocationalisation of Higher Education
15. Leadership development of educational administrators
16. Institutional restructuring and reforms
17. Capacity building and preparation, data collection and planning
18. Management of information system

The RUSA thus supports filling up of vacancies, creating new posts, faculty improvement, establishing specialized inter-university centres, innovation incubators, linkages with industries/varsities/research institutions/civil societies through PPP model so as to enhance overall quality of higher education (teaching, research and innovation). In short, RUSA is a good scheme for overall improvement of higher education as it can provide substantial financial support to HEIs.

Also, it is equally important for universities to explore linkages and collaborations with industries for specific academic programs and research projects for solving societal problems by developing new ways, and technologies, and making innovations. Offering consultancy services and running certain evening courses (e.g. personality development, teaching foreign languages, yoga & meditation, etc.) for local populace can also help generate revenue. Clearly, all members of the institution and the society at large have to strive collectively for the overall growth and development of the university and the society at large.

To sum up, judicious management of varsity finances is very important, more so for the State universities which perennially suffer from crunch of funds. Every vice chancellor should therefore take interest in learning the intricacies of finance management and guide the subordinate officials and all concerned, to ensure judicious management of every rupee earned or spent. The forgoing sections have only described major aspects of fiscal management as examples. With little involvement every university can visualize its own ingenious ways of fiscal management that are region and institution specific. Fiscal management is an art that must be addressed scientifically. So much so, the annual budget plans must not only reveal the current choices made but also reflect on how it is likely to affect the future of the institution.

Chapter 4

Curriculum: Contextualizing the Content and Delivery

Mere transaction of pre-cooked syllabi is to ignore societal purposes. Twenty-first century context must be clearly and unambiguously defined first to enable a proper designing of curriculum and reshaping of education.

The world has witnessed four major industrial revolutions (IRs 1.0-4.0) and we are currently experiencing the third wave of digital revolution. The *first wave* consisted of building the internet (1985-90) which laid foundation for the online world. The 'Internet of Things' (IoT) that is driven by the people, products, various digital platforms (e.g. Google, Amazon, etc.) all of which grew using the internet, characterized the *second wave* (2000-15). The currently on-going *third wave* is called '*Internet of Everything*'. Its ubiquitous connectivity has enabled entrepreneurs to transform almost all real-world sectors (Case, 2016). The third wave of internet has massive influence on education sector as well. Therefore, it is time to recognize the transforming value of third wave in education. In consequence, is the fact that reinvention of education requires a multifaceted approach. It is not enough to focus merely on the content: focus needs to be on context and community as well, in addition to the content. Such a focus can help universities build brands and reputation that employers value. There is no dearth of raw talent in the country. But, proper education is the key to inspire making innovations. This is the context in which the higher education systems have to function and evolve curriculum. At the same time, ensuring implementation of the curriculum in all earnestness is very important because "vision without execution is hallucination" as affirmed by America's greatest inventor Thomas Alva Edison. Thus, curriculum design and its execution are the two most important aspects of higher education institutions, especially the universities which determine the outcome; not only the fate of learners but also that of the nation as a whole. After all, the growth and sustenance of national development and international relationships rests on the quality of education imparted by the universities. The curriculum adopted in a university should ideally reflect the prevailing market pressures of the society and changing needs from time to time, and at the same time preserving the core values and cultural identities is equally important. Thanks to recent developments in science and technology, especially the digital technology and the associated *third wave* of internet the world has become a truly global village where all can express freely and influence each other. It has changed the lives of people from being the spectators to actors. This has in turn led to global citizenry. It simply means that nations can no longer stand alone in isolation. The twenty-first century curriculum of various courses and higher education system as a whole must address to issues arising out of such developments, never seen before in the history of man. Therefore, it calls for restructuring and modernizing curriculum such that it addresses the needs of this century to accomplish the global citizenship. Indeed, the twenty-first century is the most crucial moment in the history of education, especially for India and other developing countries. Higher education is the sole operating system for societal transformation: appreciation and preservation of diverse cultural identities, fight against poverty and hunger, digital, economic and social, rural-urban divides, and gender equality. Education should also focus on nurturing the culture of peace. The new curriculum must therefore have a balanced mix of sciences, arts and humanities and liberal arts through judicious integration of issues addressed by disciplines like: history, art and literature, economics, political science, sociology, philosophy, and law. Short courses on 'Contemporary History, Comparative Literature, International Economy, Constitutional Democracies and, Ethics of Human Rights' and so on should form ~25% of the total teaching hours at the graduate level as they constitute important dimensions of education globally. In addition, courses on fine arts are also needed for a multifaceted development of personality, nurture of one's passions and realization of hidden human potentials.

Universities have an undeniable role to serve as the agents of social transformation. Yet, with few exceptions they have not fulfilled their role as catalysts of social change. At the same time, with vast globalization no nation can afford to remain in the state of denial and ignorance. A defining moment for change has come in the form of twenty-first century which is poised to bring in major transformation of education systems around the world. Accordingly, India has also come up with a new education policy recently. In the process of effective implementation of NEP 2020, curriculum development is one major challenge. Furthermore, future education needs to unambiguously focus on *learning to know, learning to do, learning to live together* and *learning to be* in a social society. To this, one may add *learning to dare, dare to know* and *learn to undertake*. Therefore, the new curricula, among other things, have to wilfully aim at accomplishing global perspectives with global outlook, provide scope for mobility with supple policies, and aspects of international cooperation. Following are some ideas for curriculum development.

1. Integration of Sub-disciplines, Allied Subjects and Heralding Novel Courses

Terminologies such as 'discipline', 'intra-disciplinary', 'interdisciplinary', 'multidisciplinary', 'trans-disciplinary', 'cross-disciplinary', 'add on courses', 'open electives', are widely used but perception of these seems to differ among the academic community. Meanings of these terminologies are explained at the end of this book under the heading 'Notes'. Over the past 50 years or so, consequent to major advances in various disciplines of study, many sub-disciplines have emerged; some of these have resulted in the creation of new departments and even institutions (e.g. 'DNA Fingerprinting', 'Cell Science', etc.). But they cannot be equated with a discipline or a major subject domain. For instance, 'Biochemistry' cannot be equated to the major disciplines like the 'Biology' or 'Chemistry'. Nano-chemistry is not a discipline in itself. Likewise, 'Mathematical Modeling' is not a discipline comparable to the discipline of Mathematics or Statistics. Such examples abound across all fields of studies. Typically, the fragmentations have helped in making good progress in research and growth of the sub-disciplines and in receiving support from funding agencies. Unfortunately, there is no much crosstalk between those teaching or doing research in various sub-disciplines with the parent disciplines thereby impeding conceptualizations, consolidation and enrichment of fundamental knowledge of major subject domains.

Undeniably, in-depth understanding of a subject requires inputs from diverse disciplines, sub-disciplines and borderless areas. Moreover, rigid boundaries between the cognate subjects and disciplines have disappeared consequent to expansion and explosion of knowledge in all subject domains contributing to new understanding right at the so-called boundary levels. So much so, understanding advances made in a given subject requires basic knowledge of other disciplines. As an example, to understand the fluidity of bio-membranes one needs to understand the phenomenon of phase transition (from physical chemistry). For that matter, classical biology has now turned out to be molecular biology. Therefore, integration of classical and molecular aspects are urgently needed in all domains of biological sciences (e.g. Classical and Molecular Taxonomy; Classical and Molecular Physiology; etc.). In addition, there is a need for integration of certain components from physical sciences (e.g. biophysics, biochemistry, mathematical and statistical tools, and computer application, and so on), without which it is difficult to understand intricacies of complex biological systems. To cite other examples, integration of 'Geography', 'Geology' and 'Atmospheric Sciences' could lead to a new course: 'Earth and Atmospheric Sciences'. Physics and chemistry can possibly go together as 'Material Science'.

To give examples from Social Sciences, courses like the 'Anthropology', 'Sociology' and 'Social Works' could lead to 'Human Sciences' or under some other suitable name; separate degrees in these subjects are unwarranted. In a similar way, once considered standalone subjects like 'Economics', 'Commerce' and 'Business Management' call for integration to evolve a new course with a new name. 'History', 'Archaeology', 'Epigraphy' and 'Political Science' can go together. Such integrations are needed to transform the existing courses and meet the contemporary demands. At the same time, all researchers need to learn analytical tools of mathematics, statistics and computer science. Without adequate background knowledge of mathematical sciences it is impossible to predict the emerging patterns and trends in business or market trends, nation's GDP, demographic projections, spread of pandemics and their impacts on society and so on. Application of mathematical rigor will greatly help in analysing the data, evolving models and making projections and predictions of various kinds, and thereby enhance quality of teaching and research in social sciences. Pursuit of Indian languages with integration of Sanskrit can greatly aid in understanding the evolution of languages and promote advancements in the regional languages. In short, sweeping reforms in the curricula of UG/PG education is possible through establishing cross talks between the various sub-disciplines and disciplines. Truly cutting edge researches in most areas now require multidisciplinary approaches.

Establishing schools like: School of Physical Sciences, School of Biological Sciences, School of Languages, and School of Social Sciences, School of Liberal Arts, School of Fine Arts, and so on helps in developing an integrated approach to the study of discipline-based courses more effectively; at the same time it facilitates optimization of faculty requirements. In addition to facilitating quality training to students, it can help avoid redundancies while framing the curriculum. A school system can greatly facilitate (1) integration of subjects, (2) promotion of teaching and learning of allied subjects, and (3) undertaking research with multidisciplinary approaches. For this to happen, each university should evolve guidelines and modalities for integration of allied subjects and the working of the school system, appointment of faculty members, and so on.

To sum up this section, the courses of all programs (Arts, Science, Commerce, and Social Sciences, Engineering, Medical, Education, Law, etc.) need restructuring so as to develop new integrated courses with new titles. The traditional subject combinations at the UG studies have outlived their utility and in most cases have become uninspiring. All courses need to undergo metamorphosis; mere tinkering current curriculums here and there or offering additional subject combinations will not be of much value. Integration of relevant subjects and borderless areas is not same as providing more options. Sadly, universities are yet to undertake major transformational steps for reforming the courses at UG/PG studies. It is irrefutable that effecting major transformational changes in the curriculums we need faculty of international standings, and an enlightened and visionary leadership of the institutional heads (Vice Chancellors, Directors, and Chair Persons of BOS etc.).

As a final point, it is high time to insist on mathematical and statistical rigour across all disciplines with the exception of perhaps languages and fine arts, though students of certain biological sciences and social sciences generally show aversion to studying mathematics. Nevertheless, to strengthen higher education and production of worthy experts in various fields, taking certain hard decisions is necessary. Scientific approach is needed in learning and mastering any subject. Hopefully, the new curriculums will provide a platform for honing critical and creative thinking, solving solved and unsolved problems, and making innovations which constitute the most critical components of the twenty-first century education system at all levels.

2. Academic Flexibility

The academic flexibility involves (1) providing choice of good number of subject combinations (conventional and unconventional), (2) open electives and add on courses, (3) earn while you learn schemes, (4) flexible duration to complete the course, (5) provision for switching from one course to another (lateral entry), and (6) exit-entry options as envisaged in NEP 2020. It is necessary to weed out fixed and technically nonviable subject combinations. Mastering science as well as social science subjects requires mathematical rigor and basic knowledge of statistics. However, the curriculums must differ for different set of students. A mathematics and statistics course for various science/ social science streams may have to differ as one-hat does not fit all. For example, separate courses like 'mathematics for biological sciences', 'mathematics for physical sciences', 'mathematics for social sciences' and so on may be designed carefully. In short, these courses have to be user-specific and user-friendly. Likewise, all science disciplines require sound knowledge of basic chemistry. However, designing chemistry courses for various streams may also differ: 'chemistry for biology', 'chemistry for earth sciences', 'chemistry for physical sciences', 'chemistry for environmental studies' and so on. The universities therefore must strive to introduce such novel courses to improve and ensure better grasp of basic subjects at UG/PG levels; this will go a long way in furthering meaningful education, as envisioned in the NEP 2020.

Open electives can be highly diverse; say courses in spoken English or other foreign languages (e.g. Japanese, German, French, etc.), regional languages, Journalism, contemporary History, Tourism, Yoga & Meditation, Psychology, Contribution of Ancient Seers, Indian Society, Indian Music, Eastern philosophy, Communication skills, Skill Development, Personality Development, Entrepreneurship and Start-ups, and so on. Also, running such options as (add-on) Certificate/Diploma courses in the evenings, holidays and vacations will not only help students and members of the faculty and supporting staff of the university, but also other local populace of the city. Such courses can be on demand basis and could be run using outside experts to teach (Industries, NGOs, and Private Enterprises etc.).

Lateral entry option can become flexible provision of great consequences. If a graduate student who has not studied say English (it can be history too!) at UG level but would like to do MA in English (or History, etc.) should be able to do so if he has the ability and aptitude. Such individuals who cherish deep interest in the subject should be given a chance to appear for the entrance tests along with the others and based on their performance admission to the desired course may be made. Likewise, if a Math's or Physics graduate desires to study Economics, she/he should be welcomed. Most science graduates have the potential to excel their classmates in the broad realms of social sciences or liberal arts. Hence, flexibility in the admission process for deserving students across the faculty could be accomplished by amending the age-old archaic regulations. This requires tremendous courage, conviction and will on the part of the institutions and their leaders. Such academic flexibilities are sure to help producing experts of global standards to safeguard the interests of the country in fostering not only the science and technology, but also, country's economy, international affairs, sustainable use of environmental resources, and the very social and spiritual fabric of the country. For this to happen, quality higher education is an essential prerequisite.

Also important is to recognize the fact that in any society, at any point of time, inadequately educated workers (in various fields and domains) are found in abundance; they have few options to move up the ladder of life for want of time and resources to improve their educational qualifications and skills. Should the nation not address issues of such persons and devise ways of helping them improve their education/skills and allow their upward mobility in life? Indeed, it is possible. Universities have to evolve appropriate strategies to cover such people and give them access to higher education through suitable regulations.

Curriculum design has two additional components. First, it must include adoption of modern pedagogies and ways of assessment. Project-based learning, solving solved and unsolved problems, working in groups, participating in seminars and quizzes should become part of the new curriculum. The curriculum designers should also project model question papers and advocate for training of teachers on the logic of setting question papers such that grading of students takes place largely on its own. Assessment should focus on learner's competency gained, ability for innovation, and not on the ability for rote learning. Often one wonders whether rote learning is at the root of rot-education which has contributed to an impressive \$130 million industry of coaching classes (in India) that trains students to score high in entrance tests to enable securing seats in professional courses, and in competitive examinations to qualify for bureaucratic jobs (*Source*: https://youtu.be/8yElkAgOyqE). Alarming growth of coaching industry glaringly indicates prioritization of rote learning. Such a trend is harmful. Therefore, adopting competency-based assessment strategies is a compelling need.

A second important component of designing curriculum pertains to assessment procedures. It is safe and feasible to adopt global practices of assessment to ensure global standards. Continuous evaluation of students based on their performance in tutorials, assignments, project works, seminars, quizzes, creativity shown, ability for innovation and to work in groups and so on should suffice for awarding degrees rather than just depend on the semester-end examination. Missing the semester-end examination due to unforeseen causes like accidents, illness, pandemics, hospitalization, maternity related issues of women and so on need not cause a loss of any kind for the learners. In such unforeseen situations, based on continuous assessment and overall performance of students in the given semester, marks may be awarded. Therefore, provision of continuous rather than semester-end examination system when put in place will become a notable landmark in the history of Indian education system. It will also usher better quality of education. Evidently, learner-friendly ways of examining and awarding certificates and degrees will go a long way in fostering the interests and welfare of students.

3. Course Content and Delivery

The exercise of developing course content should begin with a clear idea of what needs to be accomplished. Therefore, some deliberation on the content, context and community (users—the industries, start-up entrepreneurs, etc.) is needed before planning for a course. Once, the content and context are clear, the universities may form a 'network of community' around it. The 'community' includes teaching faculty, industries, entrepreneurs, learners, and their long-term linkage. Such an approach can help sustain national development as well as addressing global issues. Thus, curriculum or the so-called syllabus is not a jumble of some pre-decided number of units, chosen randomly. The syllabus of a given paper has to be meaningful with the embedment of current trends and needs. It has to have a beginning and an end; encompassing elementary or historical perspectives to latest advancements in the field, with progressive increase in the complexity of concepts, from lower to higher courses. Maintaining continuity of thoughts, and relevance of knowledge gained in day-to-day life and happenings in the world around us is essential for a better appreciation of the chosen fields of studies.

It is desirable to sensitize the members of the BOS as well as the faculty about the philosophy and art of curriculum development in respect of both core and elective papers. This could be done easily through intensive discussions, seminars and lectures by experts from academia and industries before undertaking the exercise of revamping curricula for various subjects taught or proposed to be taught in a given university. Ideally, the BOS should write a brief preamble clearly stating the objectives of each paper/course and the expected outcomes.

The various Boards of Studies that prepare syllabi for high school, 10+2, UG and PG classes must have a common (subject wise) meeting to ensure continuity of thoughts and progressive increase in the complexity of ideas. Otherwise, it will result in discontinuity and disruption in the flow of thoughts. A progressive increase in the complexity of study topics as well as a proper sequencing of topics both within and between different levels is essential to guide the entire program evocatively. Each paper should have portions that depict history and evolution of the concepts, and contributions of those who are responsible for the advancement of the given field of studies/subject areas. Students should be taught on how theories are derived or arrived at, rather than merely explaining the theory. It is equally important to lay emphasis on the contributions of Indian scholars (including those residing abroad) where it is due. For instance, for us Indians, the works of the renowned Sanskrit scholar, playwright and poet Kalidasa (4th-5th CE) is more relevant than that of Shakespeare. Likewise, we need to know first our regional and Indian history, then learning the European or American history if fine; likewise, first Indian literature, then American or European literature, first Vedic mathematics and then the modern mathematics and so on. Simply stated, knowledge of local, regional and national fauna and flora, our own history and cultures and so on is more important than knowing the European, American or Australian continents. The focus of curriculum should be on a 'region and country first' approach as practiced worldwide. This will help instil confidence and national pride in the minds of learners. D.S. Kothari, the former Chairman of UGC, New Delhi held such a view very strongly and vividly articulated by saying "How can we lament lack of national pride in Indians without first acquainting them with the country's phenomenal scientific achievements in the dim distant past?" Therefore, contributions of eminent personalities in diverse fields ranging from literature, philosophy, heritage architecture, social sciences, science and technology, architecture, engineering, medicine, literature, philosophy, liberal/fine arts and so on should become part of curriculums at appropriate stages of education. In addition, to some extent focus of curriculum should be on the local and national issues, be it environment, wildlife, trade, commerce, law, history, geography and so on. It is comforting and timely to note that recently the Supreme Court Justice Shri S. Abdul Nazir said that "the need of the hour is the indigenization of the legal system" (December 27, 2021). He thus called the nation to indigenize the legal system by drawing inspiration from the ancient Indian legal philosophies and getting rid of the colonial psyche. Apparently, this calls for studying "Dharmashastra" by the legal professionals. Similar calls are also warranted in respect of Mathematics, Ayurveda, India's ancient cultures, ethos and so on. It is equally important that school and college curriculums incorporate components of health and public hygiene, civic sense, and importance of honesty and integrity in social life and building the nation. At the same time, curriculums across the disciplines must succeed in conveying that no nation can progress or become eminently humane when large mass of people remain unemployed, under privileged and do not have access even to clean water and clean air. Equity and access have to be accomplished for all as far as the basic needs are concerned.

Lastly, curriculum so set, should display enough flexibility and scope for experimentation and innovation within an overall program structure to let incorporation of new developments and or deletion of some portions as may be needed from time to time. Ideally, there should be scope for allowing the curricula for their own revisions and on-going improvements. The curricular designs of various courses should also provide directions for teaching, procurement of human material and fiscal resources to implement the envisioned programs. As an example, there can be a clear direction that a given paper be taught by a single teacher (instead of dividing the units between two or more teachers) so that teaching can occur sequentially. An added benefit is that it will help improve domain knowledge of the course teachers and their accountability. Lastly, any curriculum once framed must undergo the process of updating as often as needed based on objective evaluation and assessment of outcomes. This will facilitate undertaking corrective measures.

4. Creating Faculty Positions to Sustain New Courses

Consequent to integration of sub-disciplines and borderless areas teaching becomes a major problem due to the inadequacy of trained faculty. The existing faculty may find it difficult to manage modernized curricula with integration of areas from related domains. For instance, in biological sciences like the zoology, botany, microbiology, an important course pertains to "Taxonomy and Biosystematics". Such a course is very important in the management of country's biodiversity and its conservation. However, classical taxonomy is not enough anymore. We need to incorporate molecular taxonomy and develop a new course such as the 'Classical and Molecular Taxonomy and Systematics'. Similarly, a forceful emergence of areas like the 'Molecular Cell Biology', 'Molecular Genetics', 'Integrated Molecular Physiology', 'Systems Biology' and so on necessitate creation of new faculty positions because such courses require experts who can teach both theory and devise laboratory exercises. Similar situations prevail with respect to other science (e.g. Drug designing, immune-pharmacology, nano-science, etc.) as well as social science subjects and fine arts.

In the past, many universities used to run specialized courses (e.g. Spectroscopy, Nuclear Chemistry, Biophysics, Entomology, Genetics, Comparative Endocrinology, International Economics, Archaeology, Epigraphy, etc.) based on the expertise and research of faculty members. After these faculty members retired, often it has resulted in the closure of such subject domains. Therefore, in most universities specializations have progressively disappeared as they were not sustained by recruitment of appropriate faculty in the concerned subject domain. The regulatory agencies like the UGC must ponder over such developments and evolve appropriate strategies to revive quality teaching and research in both core and specialized domains. Blind adherence to faculty-student ratio (FSR) can be disastrous to higher education and research in universities. Coming back to the philosophy enshrined in the NEP 2020, in most situations, the current faculty will find it difficult to accomplish integration of intra disciplinary courses or undertake research in such areas. At the same time, new areas continue to emerge from time to time, e.g. nano-science, nano-biology, polymer science, Mathematical Biology, Mathematical Modeling, Corporate Social Responsibility, International Trade and Business, International Law, AI, and so on. Teaching and research in new branches require state of the art expertise in the given subject domain. Unarguably, therefore, the regulatory bodies that control HEIs (colleges and universities) must first facilitate creation of new faculty positions for each subject domain keeping in mind the specific courses taught in a given university department. This will help them take forward the major objectives of NEP 2020: (i) redesigning new courses through integration of allied fields, and (ii) use of multidisciplinary approach in research. Unfortunately, at present in most colleges and universities the teaching programs are run by the unemployed guest faculty on contractual basis regardless of their competency to teach a given subject. The UGC/universities should identify the core papers taught in each department and qualifications of teachers required to teach those courses. Gone are the days where anyone could teach any subject. For example, a taxonomist is ill qualified to teach advances in physiology or genetics. Many such examples can be given for all disciplines. In any case, quality teaching and research at colleges and universities cannot be sustained long and meaningfully with ad-hoc arrangements. Therefore, subject-designated faculty positions for *core* and *specialized* courses should be created and appointments made in a given university. Mere maintaining faculty-student ratio (FSR) is meaningless if it does not cater to the needs of teaching diverse subjects that make a discipline,

An important issue in teaching-learning process especially in science subjects is hands-on training in laboratories. Therefore, to strengthen such training a few positions of Assistant Professors (*Research and Laboratory*) in each science department need creation; such faculty can engage in setting up good labs, conducting practical classes, introducing new exercises periodically, supervising field/project works and producing laboratory manuals. Such teachers can be given a running scale with suitably defined efficiency bars for promotion. Such teachers need not be part of the rat-race to publish papers in predatory journals. A primary job of such teachers is imparting practical knowledge, teaching creative learning, critical thinking and problem solving. They may also carry out some research as well. However, the criteria for promotion or salary enhancement of such teachers may be based on their performance in fostering laboratory teaching, promotion of skill development, critical and creative thinking, introduction of new exercises, preparing laboratory manuals, handling and maintaining laboratory equipment, and so on but not research publication per se. With such changes one can hope to inspire students to become skilled as well as good scientists of the future (Saidapur, 2017).

5. Redesigning Classrooms

The modern education system envisages drastic changes in the pedagogies of teaching-learning-assessment processes. Hence, the new curricula should also specify various requirements like the equipment, software, virtual labs, models and other facilities with respect to each course in detail to facilitate their acquisition and installation without undue delay. The new requirements predominantly involve adoption of several digital technologies and online platforms of learning, MOOCs, virtual labs, several apps, and specific software extensively. Hence, every classroom has to be redesigned to facilitate adoption of new pedagogies and modern gadgets of learning and high-speed Wi-Fi facilities. The teachers and learners themselves have to be equipped with the modern gadgets like computers, tablets or smart phones and needed training to use them. In the changed scenario one can imagine that in future, teachers will have predominantly a facilitating role. They will no more be a sage on the stage, but a guide on the side. In accordance with the changing scenario of teaching-learning pedagogies, the assessment system will also change to incorporate aspects for testing the outcomes and competency of learners for creativity and innovation rather than ability for memory-based learning.

Lastly, the Karnataka Science and Technology Academy (KSTA has brought out a policy paper on "Revamping Science Education in Karnataka" recently under the chairmanship of this author which is in sync with the NEP 2020. It can come handy in understanding the philosophy and intricacies of framing curriculums in science subjects and promotion of research. Similarly, the State Governments or the universities can get such policy papers prepared for other major subjects with the help of experts in social sciences, liberal and fine arts, and languages for adoption in the UG/PG programs.

6. Preparation of Books and Manuals

In view of the NEP 2020, course contents of all subjects are poised to metamorphose with integration of multiple areas hitherto studied separately, paving way for better conceptualization of fundamentals, gaining competency to handle new challenges and undertake multidisciplinary approach in research. Therefore, new books and manuals (laboratory exercises) are needed by both students and teachers to quickly adopt newer ways of teaching-learning-assessment processes. It is therefore very desirable for universities to solicit preparation of study materials (books and manuals) in tune with the new curriculums from eminent scholars to write individually or in collaboration (co-opting experts where needed) with their counterparts (experts from multidisciplinary domains, superannuated teachers/researchers) from the same or other premier institutions. The books could be published by the universities themselves.

To sum up, considerable efforts are need to transform the existing curricula into new integrated and fully metamorphosed structures for both UG and PG courses for paving way to quality higher education. Espousal of currently relevant course contents in relation to the context that is built around the community of entrepreneurs on one hand, and modern pedagogies of teaching-learning processes on the other, will paint our universities in good light. Furthermore, it is crucial to realize that curriculum is not merely about completing syllabus; universities and colleges must strive to provide treasure of campus experience that alumni can fondly remember lifelong. For instance, organizing a day of 'donations' enabling students, faculty and supporting staff as well as local citizens to make their offerings (in cash or kind) and the amount collected can be given to orphanages, meeting unforeseen calamities like the Covid-19 related issues, deluge, earthquakes, forest fires, defence services and so on depending upon the exigency. Such events should be organized annually and help mitigate sufferings of fellow beings. The universities with its huge strength of students, faculty, supporting staff and alumni can easily adopt orphanages in the town and support the real needy segment of the society. Going a step further, universities and colleges can solicit ideas from stakeholders themselves and certain needy organizations. Involvement of universities in the wellbeing of the society can help gain high credibility for itself. The campus experience should help in molding the personality and convictions of the learners, generate national pride, and empathy for fellow human beings. Creating a good humane society is the ultimate aim of education and the universities must play a frontier role in this process. Curriculum so designed must address the above issues as forcefully as possible.

Chapter 5

Promotion of Germane Research

A good researcher will aim at generating new knowledge, making innovation or resolving societal problems and in the process nurture her/his own passion.

Ideally, research should become an important activity of all universities. It is through publication of research findings in globally reputed journals, guiding students to undertake original researches, tackling unsolved fundamental problems or contributing to development of new technology and/or innovations, and publication of quality books the universities build their own reputation and ranking. Therefore, it is imperative that the universities engage themselves in the attainment of higher and higher distinctions through scholarly output in research, publication of books, monographs, laboratory manuals, other study materials, and establish credibility of their credentials (utility value of certificates) firmly. Furthermore, the universities also need to serve as the 'think tanks' of the nation. Provided academic freedom the academics can play a significant role in building a sound education system, science and technology base, evolution of policies in all spheres of human activities like growth and sustenance of economy, trade and commerce, law and order, protection of environment and sustainable utilization of environmental resources, health and hygiene, international relationships, defence, building bridges between the haves and have not, and a harmonious society to name a few. The universities must contribute to expertise of global standards in all spheres of human endeavours needed for sustenance of nations. Therefore, need based, relevant, and original research works should be undertaken in areas of contemporary interest and thereby enrich human lives around the world. The ultimate aim of universities is to facilitate fulfilment of aspirations of the people. If the universities fail; the nations fail.

Highest standards of education system and culture of innovation are absolutely essential for development of nations. Hence, in order to sustain quality research (various spheres), relevant to the national growth, the universities must attract and recruit eminent faculty drawn nationally and even globally from wherever, and whenever possible because reputation of the universities depends largely or solely on the teaching and research activities. It is widely believed that those who cannot do good research have nothing to teach. Thus, it is quite imperative that the institutions and their heads proactively support academic activities of the faculty.

Innovative researches often depend largely on the infrastructure, competency, and commitment of the personnel involved in research, the faculty and students. At the same time, vibrant, competitive, and congenial academic ecosystem are essential for the sustenance of cutting-edge research and overall academic growth. In this process, the academic leadership of the vice chancellors and the governing bodies play a pivotal role. All that the university has to do is to reduce bureaucracy, speed up clearance of files, and allow smooth operation of research funds. Researchers procure grants from R&D agencies for their research projects but they often face difficulties in utilizing the sanctioned funds. Too many hassles and too many procedures that one has to follow can discourage faculty members from procuring R&D grants. Obtaining 'Utilization Certificates' on time and facing mundane audit objections can be a real pain in the neck for an academician. Consequently, many researchers either do not seek funding or unable to utilize fully the sanctioned amount due to unfriendly procedures that involve chasing files for administrative approvals, placing orders, drawing advances, settling accounts, dealing with inane audit objections and so on. The university should seriously look into the problems of researchers and make operation of R&D grants simple and provide user-friendly rules for utilizing funds. The universities should proactively initiate steps to promote both teaching and research. Following are some strategies that will help researchers and promote research in a significant way.

1. Central Instrumentation Facility with Qualified Technicians

For science departments, a central facility like 'University Science Instrumentation Centre' (USIC) plays an indispensable role in supporting the researchers. However, there should be good number of instruments and qualified technicians so that the researchers can carry out their work easily. For this, the university must have adequate funds and a mechanism in place to enable procurement of needed equipment, glassware and chemicals promptly. The USIC should be funded on priority basis by the UGC and also the university by creating separate budgetary provision (Budget Head). Overhead grants of R&D projects may be pooled to support smooth functioning of USIC.

Furthermore, universities with central instrumentation facility should evolve policies to ensure that all costly equipment procured under various R&D grants by researchers of different departments are placed there for use by all researchers of the institution. Proper maintenance of various scientific instruments should be ensured through appropriate 'Annual Maintenance Contracts'. Also universities should provide technicians for operation of sophisticated instruments. Such centres can also offer (1) analytical services to researchers from other institutions and industries and earn some revenue, (2) a course on instrumentation to research scholars, and (3) a short course on statistical applications in research to research scholars and faculty members.

2. Research Director

In order to promote and facilitate research works of various departments it is a good idea to have a full time Research Director, a senior professor (from science faculty) who can play the role of a liaison officer between the university authorities and the USIC. Alternatively, a superannuated professor with sound research background (an experimentalist) can also be appointed by outsourcing on a fixed monthly honorarium. The research director should also inspire and motivate the young faculty to undertake research not only in their area but also in interdisciplinary areas. This can be done through organizing short lecture workshops of 2-3 days for researchers of the university and inviting eminent resource persons to deliver talks in different faculties. An outcome-based performance can be the basis of continuance of the Research Directors. Their performance could be reviewed annually.

3. Promotion of Multidisciplinary Approach in Research

Sharp boundaries between allied subjects that once existed have blurred necessitating multidisciplinary approach in research. For example, predicting and modelling business trends, making demographic projections, economic trends, GDP, inflation, spread of pandemics and so on requires sound knowledge of mathematics and statistics. When combined with commerce and business management the pursuit of economics leads to more meaningful and useful results. Similarly, integration of sociology, social work, and anthropology can provide better understanding of the human behaviour and evolution. This will in turn, help in a better management of human societies (tribal, rural and urban etc.). This is also true of modern Indian languages. Sanskrit is the operating system on which most Indian languages have evolved; Tamil may be an exception but it also has large number of Sanskrit words in it. In any case, study of languages when coupled with the mother language (Sanskrit) promotes a deeper and better understanding of the literature. Besides, the Dravidian languages like Malayalam, Kannada and Telugu have grown by liberally accepting Sanskrit words.

In the science domains also boundaries between the allied subjects have disappeared greatly calling for their judicious integration to understand the intricacies and enable cutting edge researches. Classic example is biological science. Basic knowledge of all other science disciplines is needed to understand complex organization of biological forms. Today, without sound basic knowledge of allied subjects it is almost impossible to carry out state of the art research in any branch of science or social sciences. Therefore, adoption of multi sided approach to research is indispensible; importance of such a strategy needs little emphasis.

4. Promotion of Linkages and Collaborations

Current focus of education and research is on multidisciplinary approach that calls for collaboration and linkage with other researchers from the same institution as well as from premier institutions and industries. A multidisciplinary approach can start with inter-departmental collaborations within the university itself because a quality research is no longer possible in isolation. Moreover, in science subjects most modern, costly equipment and sophisticated facilities are needed for cutting-edge research. Most universities do not afford to have their own facilities for cutting-edge research. Linkage and collaborations can help overcome institutional deficiencies (e.g. sophisticated and costly equipment) in a big way. So, universities should proactively encourage and facilitate linkages with industries, and premier institutions in India and abroad through appropriate mechanisms and properly designed memorandum of understanding (MOU). In most universities, even intradepartmental collaborations are not visible. Hence, first step would be to start with inter and intra departmental collaborations within the university and extend them to inter institutional collaborations. Such progressive initiatives can also help enhancing quality research in the given subject area.

5. Adjunct and Visiting Professors

The universities should evolve provisions to appoint adjunct and visiting professors from premier institutions and industries with established track records, from India and/or abroad and engage them for teaching, research and collaborations. This will go a long way in strengthening the academic milieu of the institution. Eminent scientists, educationists and experts from Arts and humanities or liberal arts can also be engaged as adjunct/ visiting professors to strengthen the PG departmental activities. For all these, suitable mechanisms may have to be evolved by each institution.

6. Research Mentor

It is necessary that researchers understand the very purpose and need for quality research. They must know the difference between repetitive research and original research. Research must contribute to creation of new knowledge in the fundamental area of the subject or make innovations or help in resolving specific local/national societal problems. Mere production of unworthy researchers and doctoral degrees based on mundane, repetitive research works is a futile exercise at the cost of tax payers. Such works need to be sternly discouraged as it also brings bad name to the institution, research supervisors and the candidates themselves. The universities may actually have formal mechanisms to ensure that mundane and repetitive research works are not undertaken by its faculty. An eminent mentor could be appointed to oversee research topics by the students, for a fixed duration of say 3-5 years. The chosen mentor should be an eminent academician or an industrialist of known repute. Quality research can be fostered in two ways: (1) through voluntary action of researchers themselves; this will happen provided good faculty is recruited, and (2) when the faculty fails to contribute to useful research, mentoring and use of strict promotion criteria could bring out desired results. Academically poor faculty may however protest under the garb of 'academic freedom'. Therefore, if at least 50% of faculty is of high quality in each PG department, the situation may still be bearable as the academic divisions will still remain viable and relevant. Therefore, every new vice chancellor should be given a freedom to invite highly competent and academically eminent academicians (say 5% of faculty) from India or abroad to fill the faculty positions. For this to happen, first condition is that the concerned governments appoint a good vice chancellor with honesty and integrity. Given academic freedom such vice chancellors will enhance the academic environment of the institution. In any case, carefully thought-out strategies are needed to improve quality of doctoral research that is original, relevant and meaningful.

7. Renaming Doctoral Theses as 'Dissertations'

It is a fact now that most theses submitted in Indian universities do not contain a '*Thesis*' *per se*. It generally contains experimental or survey data. Besides, the doctoral students undergo course works and the research carried out by the candidates by way of collecting data based on experiments, literature study or surveys using questionnaires and preparing a compendium towards the partial fulfilment, for obtaining the doctoral degree. Calling such documents that adore libraries as *theses* can be embarrassing. More often than not, most doctoral students and their supervisors fail to understand true meaning of thesis. It is safe to call such compendiums of doctoral research works as '*Dissertation*'. This is more appropriate now that M.Phil. program is abolished which used to have a dissertation.

8. Professional Ethics: Curbing Plagiarism

In any society, ideals are voluntarily followed by a few individuals. When the ideal activity (say doing research) is institutionalized as it happened after the 19th century, the *ideal state* can be ensured only through reward/punishment system. The ethical guidelines of CSIR recommend establishment of an 'Office of Research Integrity' with an Ombudsman to monitor unethical practices. A similar mechanism is needed for educational institutions engaged in conducting research. May be the regulatory bodies that control/govern universities should evolve such mechanisms.

Academic integrity in research is very important. Profession in scientific pursuits by itself must teach honesty and integrity; after all science is global. Also, universities should no more allow repetitive researches and publication in predatory journals, using well defined mechanisms. Professional ethics should be respected and followed at all costs (see Chaddah, 2019; Muralidhar et al., 2019 for an exhaustive coverage of the topic). In recent times, considerable malpractices, plagiarism have surfaced among the research community leading to retraction of published papers published in high impact factor journals even by the researchers of premier institutions. This is very unfortunate and demoralizing to the entire research community. Besides, hurting the reputation of the concerned researchers, it affects the reputation of the institution. Therefore, universities and for that matter all research institutions should have mechanisms to identify such unforgivable acts of malpractices like data theft, data copying, copy text/ plagiarism, and punish those involved in such unethical practices. Punishment should be no less than dismissal from service of those indulging in professionally unethical practices. Further, research students during their course works should be sensitized about the importance of honesty and integrity in research, as well as about the adverse and unpleasant consequences of malpractice. University teachers do have an obligation to undertake quality research; it is said, he who does not research, has nothing to teach.

9. Creating Provision of Seed Money

When a new faculty is appointed he/she needs initial support from the institution to build the basic facilities needed for undertaking research by way of seed money. This may include financial support to build a laboratory, preparation of grant proposals, and travel support for presenting grant proposals before the funding agency. Ideally, all new faculty members should be supported for the initial period of 3-5 years. The support can be to the extent of 5-10 Lakh depending upon the need, project proposal, capability and potential/track record of the investigator and institutional soundness of finances. The Central Government funded varsities and a certain premier research and teaching institutions have provision in place for providing the seed money. This is generally lacking in State universities, with few exceptions if any. Therefore, the concerned State Governments should provide separate grants as seed money to universities.

10. Central Library

A good central library with latest books and access to national and international journals in various fields will go a long way in promoting research and pursuit of scholarly activities. The library ambience should also be pleasant so that the readers feel like spending more time there. Since it is impossible to provide large number of periodicals, the libraries may subscribe to e-journals and various e-portals. In addition, good reprography facility should be in place. Libraries could even download articles on request and email to researchers and collect nominal charges.

In addition to the aforesaid, universities now need to evolve ways of promoting reading habits and attracting students and faculty to spend time in libraries in view of the weaning reading habit among them. This is indeed a big challenge. Yet, the libraries need to develop innovative ways of catering to the needs of researchers, students, and teachers so that they remain relevant and not redundant in the on-going and rapidly progressing digital era. The recent descriptions by Joshi (2019) and Sathyanarayana (2019) deliberate elegantly on the evolution of digital libraries, and library as the learning resource. These articles could be consulted for required orientation of university Librarians.

11. Sparing Faculty Members from Mundane Works

Often the varsity professors are given tasks outside their academic realms. These include: looking after the Hostels, Gymkhana, NCC, NSS, Sports Section, Youth Festivals, and various types of jobs connected with the extracurricular nature like: the 'Dean, Student's welfare; Director, College Development Cell; Planning and Development Officer' to name a few obvious ones. In addition professors, who have no academic commitments or love for teaching, gleefully aspire to serve as the Registrar or Registrar Evaluation. Therefore, there needs to be a strategy in place to spare teachers from involving them for non-academic activities. On the other hand, teachers need to be on various committees (e.g. Admission Committee, Library Committee, USIC, Purchase Committee, Academic Council, Senate, Syndicate and such other committees) of the universities and help promote academic growth and development of the institution. These assignments do not affect teaching and research significantly. At the same time, serving on such committees helps in gaining good insights about the functioning of the university. Hence these assignments are welcome.

12. Rewarding Good Researchers

Each university may evolve its own strategies of appreciation and awards to the deserving researchers who publish papers in reputed journals or receive prestigious awards and recognitions at the State/National and international levels, prestigious fellowships to go abroad for collaborative research, or as visiting scientist. The awards should be in the form of say a letter of appreciation from the head of the institution, additional grants for research, honorary doctoral degrees (depending upon the nature of recognition received—Gyan Peeth award, Padma awards, Shanti Swarup Bhatnagar Prize, etc.) and so on but not cash awards. It is to show that the parent institution recognises the good work done by its students/faculty and motivate them for further contribution in the field of teaching and research. At the same time, universities may have mechanisms to punish the underperformers and undesirable performers by withholding increments and promotions, extending probation period and so on.

13. Formulating User Friendly Rules for Operation of Funds

Most State universities are generally not in a position to entirely support the investigators by providing state of the art infrastructure, laboratory facilities and meet the day-to-day running expenditures and scholarships to research students. Hence, researchers invariably need to secure funding from various R&D agencies of India and also from abroad. However, getting funds is one thing, using it is another. Often the institutional rules and regulations that are old and archaic, formulated with colonial ruler's mind set, are too stringent, bureaucratic, time consuming and full of hassles that discourage investigators from seeking research grants. Having realized this, some universities have liberalized the rules. One such university is the Karnatak University which imaginatively evolved 'User-friendly Guidelines for Operation of Research Grants' over a decade ago, in the year 2007 (see Appendix 3). This eliminated bureaucracy and enhanced comfort of operating the research grants. As a result, in the subsequent years, more and more faculty members sought and received research funding and there was a notable increase in the number of grants received by the faculty. In a similar way, it is also possible for all other universities/institutions to evolve similar guidelines with even more liberalization to encourage investigators to bring in more funds. Utility of such reforms is truly enormous. When operating research grants becomes simple and easy, the investigators can concentrate on research rather than on file management and spend time in chasing the approvals and so on. Likewise, the audit process needs to be quick and least cumbersome. It is possible to easily resolve this issue by permitting the use of University approved list of Chartered Accountants to audit research funds and issue utilization certificates.

In summary, promotion of germane research will go a long way in promoting quality of teaching and research as well as building brand for universities. Good research does not always cost money; it often requires change of mind-set, encouragement, competitive academic ecosystem and a user-friendly administration. Furthermore, in the face of the changing global compulsions, universities ought to nurture talent and facilitate tackling unsolved scientific or societal problems, and developing the culture of innovations that ultimately lead to self-reliance (*Atmanirbhar*). Going a step further, unethical practices and plagiarisms that harm the reputation of individuals as well as the institutions must be curbed at all costs.

Chapter 6

Management of Constituent and Affiliated Colleges

University run constituent colleges must serve as the models to affiliated colleges to enable advancement and expansion of higher education in the region.

The First Grade Degree Colleges are all affiliated to the university in their region which awards degrees to students of affiliated institutions. Thus, the State universities cater to the needs of large number of affiliated colleges; sometimes as many as 500 or even more. Such universities have a gargantuan work and responsibility of finely regulating academic programs and their implementation in both constituent and affiliated colleges. This includes, providing curriculums for various courses, setting question papers, conducting examinations and evaluation of answer papers, declaring results and issuing marks cards and certificates to name a few. As a rule, the affiliating universities are overburdened. In addition, the State universities also run their own colleges (constituent colleges) in different faculties like the arts, science and humanities, engineering, medical, law, commerce, management, education and so on. An underlying principle of running constituent colleges is to run them as 'Model' Colleges, provide guidance to affiliated colleges and show them how to run a college in most befitting ways. However, constituent colleges have rarely attained the distinction of being model colleges. On the contrary, there are numerous instances where the private colleges and even government colleges outclass the university run constituent colleges by providing better quality infrastructure, teaching faculty and education. The affiliation system is not followed in more advanced western countries. The system of affiliation in a way is now out-dated.

The widely debated National Education Policy (NEP 2020) among other things recommends discontinuation of the system of affiliation of colleges over a period of next 15 years. However, disaffiliation and making the colleges fully autonomous is not easy. Numerous challenges will surface. In any case, the universities will have to manage the affiliated colleges for next 15 years at the least or even more depending upon the progress of disaffiliation processes. However, the constituent colleges will remain with the parent universities providing UG programs or integrated UG-PG programs. Overall management of colleges was recently described in detail (Saidapur, 2019abc). This chapter focuses on the envisioned role of universities with respect to the constituent and affiliated colleges running under their purview.

A. Constituent Colleges

As stated before, by implication it is imperative that the constituent colleges serve as the model institutions, lest there is no hope for elevating standards of other colleges in the region (Government or Private). Furthermore, poorly run constituent colleges and PG departments are likely to have a degrading influence on other HEIs in the region. As the constituent colleges are run directly by the university the stakeholders expect that infrastructure and performance of such colleges to be better than other colleges in the region. The constituent colleges therefore need to maintain high academic standards reflected in the curriculum and its delivery, choice of core courses, electives, add-on courses, and best practices followed. If so, they can provide leadership to other colleges in the region. It is with this perspective; the universities must give great attention to their constituent colleges and make them exemplary. Unfortunately, in most cases the constituent colleges differ little from the affiliated colleges on all parameters like the quality and performance of teaching staff, infrastructure, academic flexibility, option of core and open electives, choice of modern interdisciplinary courses, and best practices. Consequently, they hardly inspire the affiliated colleges nor they are in a position to provide leadership. More often than not, the universities merely struggle to control the affiliated colleges without giving much needed guidance. The State Governments should take necessary steps to upgrade constituent colleges of all universities (as long as they continue affiliation system and even after that) and transform them into 'model colleges' that private colleges can emulate and gain considerably. The experiments, expertise and experience of constituent colleges can then serve as exemplars for replication by other colleges around with confidence and courage. The constituent colleges should develop appropriate strategies and procedures for adopting modern pedagogies; ways of conducting and assessing the performance of students in seminars, quizzes, execution of projects, home assignments, ability to learn in groups and self-learning and so on. Use and standardization of modern pedagogies in the constituent colleges can greatly help inspire other colleges to adopt the same with ease. In fact, experimentation with new courses and new pedagogies and their outcome can become very useful for other colleges in the region and the State. Success stories of the constituent colleges will go a long way in inspiring the affiliated, autonomous-private or government colleges. Therefore, constituent colleges should become pioneers in the introduction of (1) new courses, (2) new and unconventional subject combinations, (3) integrated and modernized courses, (4) open electives, (5) add-on courses, (6) novel provisions for horizontal mobility across courses, (7) personality development courses, (8) mentoring and counselling students, (9) promotion of skill development and entrepreneurship, (10) innovative and best practices, (11) harnessing the potential of alumni association, (12) institution of endowments, (13) 'earn while you learn' schemes, (14) e-governance, (15) user-friendly administration, (16) promotion of sports, cultural and social activities, (17) ensuring outcome-based teaching learning processes, (18) making green campus, (19) enhancing employability and entrepreneurship, and (20) preparing future ready graduates with needed skills. More importantly, recognizing the transformative value and impact of the 'third wave' of internet or the so-called 'internet of everything' on the future education systems from schools to universities is an urgent need. Constituent colleges of universities are thus best suited to undertake transformation of collegiate education in their region.

Evidently, universities need to redesign the style of running their constituent colleges and provide proper guidance and leadership. Lastly, in redesigning university colleges it is imperative that philosophy enshrined in the NEP 2020 is considered earnestly.

B. Affiliated Colleges

In India, colleges imparting UG/PG education are all affiliated to universities located in their region. Affiliation means association, relationship, connection, attachment and membership. Obviously, once a college is affiliated to a university, all these terms apply automatically. It is a relationship which must yield measurable results in terms of production of quality products by the college. To accomplish the desired results, the universities must go beyond collecting prescribed fee of various kinds and granting the membership/affiliation to colleges. An affiliating university must guide, help and ensure that the colleges perform well. Unfortunately, such a philosophy is not strongly embedded in the maxim of universities. In reality, universities largely indulge in sending their team of professors periodically to inspect and submit reports on granting new or continuation of affiliation, increasing or decreasing student intake to a given course, approvals to start new courses, or allowing closure of demand-less courses. Ideally, the visit of Local Inquiry Committees (LICs) to the affiliated institutions should be user-friendly and educative in nature. But, often we hear the murmur that the committees visiting especially the professional colleges harass the college managements. To avoid such embarrassments, transparent mechanisms and specific guidelines may be provided by the affiliating university to both members of the LIC and the colleges. The 'Guidelines for Local Inquiry Committee' should be explicit with a preamble and suggestions to both the committee members and the colleges. The author had issued such guidelines during his tenure as VC at K.U. Dharwad. A sample of such guidelines is given below.

Guidelines for LIC Members

1. First, the members should acquaint and become conversant with the conditions prescribed for fresh, temporary and permanent affiliations. The Chairperson

of the LIC may brief the members about their responsibilities before the start of the visit.

2. The committee should verify the documents pertaining to the payment of dues (various forms of fees to be sent to the university including the reimbursement amount in respect of SC/ST/OBC students by the college and, report to the university.
3. The LIC members should also interact with the teaching and non-teaching staff and students separately to record their complaints if any and suggestions which can be brought to the notice of the Principal/Management for corrective actions.
4. The committee should carefully consider the reports of previous LIC visits before recommending continuation of affiliation or disaffiliation and ensure consistency between succeeding reports.
5. The assessment should be fair, transparent and objective giving no scope for complaints or ambiguities.
6. Recommendations should be based on academic ground; avoid making recommendations as ‘special cases’.
7. The report should also highlight noteworthy developments of the institution and innovative measures taken for all-round development of students if any.
8. Proactive role of the Principal/Management, if any, should be highlighted. Likewise, incompetence of the Principal, if apparent, may also be highlighted in a subtle way.
9. The committee, in no uncertain terms, should discourage the management from extending unwarranted embarrassing hospitalities during its visit.
10. Lastly, the visiting committees should take cognizance of the previous reports and recommendations made by the ranking institutions like the NAAC and NIRF etc.

Guidelines for Colleges

1. All relevant documents should be made available to committee members for verification.

2. The Principal should seek as much information as possible from the LIC members regarding the new initiatives taken by the university and regulatory bodies. Also they may facilitate interaction of students and staff members with visiting LIC.
3. The Principal may provide feedback (confidential or otherwise) to the Vice-Chancellor/Registrar directly by email or through a letter within 24 hours of the visit of LIC. The Principal may briefly state his/her observations on the nature of interaction (usefulness, pleasant or unpleasant, etc.) with the visiting members.
4. The Principal should restrain from providing any special treatment (flowers, etc.) to the visiting committee that may be construed as efforts to please the committee. Formal functions shall not be arranged. The LIC visit shall be treated as an occasion for showcasing the academic achievements of the institution and for seeking needed permissions from the affiliating university. No more, no less.
5. In case of fresh affiliation for starting a college or seeking extension of courses, the members of the management shall invariably be present at the time of inspection and interact with the LIC.

The LICs are meant to assess the potential of the college and management for undertaking proposed programs like starting a new college, continuation of affiliation to the university, increase in student intake and so on based on the availability of infrastructure, financial soundness, academic environment, local needs, and overall capability of the college management for good governance.

Lastly, though the system of affiliation is supposed to be discontinued as per the recommendation of NEP 2020 in the coming years implementation of new policies and successes largely depend upon the carefully thought-out strategies of the concerned universities, higher education councils and concerned institutions and the State Governments. Therefore, the affiliating universities must begin discussion with the colleges and in statutory bodies and then evolve specific strategies. Developing a proper *modus operandi* for smooth transition from affiliating to non-affiliating status of colleges obviously requires well-drawn plans that are mutually agreeable between colleges and the university.

C. Management of Collegiate Education

Managing collegiate education is indeed a huge task (Saidapur, 2019). Highest number of graduates comes out of colleges which are now affiliated but in the near future they are set to be disaffiliated. Hence, proper management of collegiate education attains paramount importance. In many states collegiate education is typically managed by Director of Collegiate Education who is a senior principal of a government degree college or by the Commissioner of Collegiate Education who may be even a bureaucrat. Both these arrangements suffer from certain inherent drawbacks. One such drawback is inadequate academic background. Apparently, the Department of Collegiate Education has to manage academic and administrative domains of disaffiliated/autonomous colleges run by the government or the private managements. In addition, implementation of NEP 2020 is a major challenge of the colleges/universities with far and wide consequences. Undoubtedly, management of collegiate education needs leadership of great vision and high calibre.

The collegiate education is very important and it needs a meticulous planning and a road map. It must proactively resonate with the needs of the changing demographic scenarios of the society. Ideally, management of collegiate education should be in the hands of visionary academicians. Uninspiring management using inexperienced bureaucrats who are naive in matters of higher education and often possess no vision for its growth and expansion leads to disastrous outcome. Most bureaucrats do not evince much interest in such postings and seek quick transfers to other lucrative positions. Ideally, an academician of high accomplishments should head the Department of Collegiate Education and have the same status as the vice chancellor of a university. Filling up such a position should follow open advertisement inviting applications by prescribing needed basic qualification. The qualifications should include research experience, handling research projects sanctioned by the R&D agencies and experience in collaboration/

linkage with premier institutions and or industries. The short-listed candidates must compulsorily give a power point presentation highlighting their vision and mission, priorities and plans (say for next 5 years) for revitalizing collegiate education before the search/selection committee. Further, it is good to invite some principals of premier colleges for interaction with the shortlisted candidates. The committee may interact in depth with the potential candidates to assess their competency, vision, and mission, and then choose the best.

Some State Governments have instituted a 'Higher Education Academy' for training the newly recruited college teachers with a view to provide orientation. Such academies can also involve in training teachers on issues like the curriculum development, adoption of modern pedagogies of teaching, learning, and assessment, and concept of continuous assessment, executing project works, solving solved and unsolved problems, teaching creative and critical thinking, working in groups, and counselling and mentoring the students, and so on through workshops and short-term courses. Thus, the Higher Education Academies can indirectly support implementation of NEP 2020 instead of being mere onlookers.

In summary, the affiliating universities and concerned government departments must take the management of constituent and affiliated colleges seriously such that outcome becomes visible and measurable. Even after the cessation of affiliating system, in the foreseeable or distant future, the role of State governments will remain the same or even become more crucial. At the same time, the universities should continue to provide higher order leadership to collegiate education by (1) transforming their own constituent colleges as models, and (2) guiding all the colleges in the region. Lastly, the colleges will require mentoring in a big way. Therefore, they may utilize services of eminent academicians (in service or superannuated) with established track record as the institutional mentors. The institutions can change the mentors once in five years or so. The mentoring process is clearly and solely to promote pursuit of excellence in higher education.

Chapter 7

Repurposing the Centres of Human Resource Development

> *Quality human resource development will prove to be a key issue for any nation for its all-round development, sustainability and meeting the local, national and global challenges in future.*

'Academic Staff Colleges' (ASC) were established by the UGC in the year 1986 in some chosen universities. Subsequently, they were renamed as 'Human Resource Development Centers' (HRDC) in the year 2015. The mandate of HRDCs is to train the newly recruited as well as in-service faculty members of universities and colleges. They offer mainly two types of courses: the 'Orientation Course' and 'Refresher Course' often referred as OC and RC respectively. These are of three weeks duration. The objectives of HRDCs and the terms OCs and RCs are clearly defined. In addition to such colleges, some States have established 'Higher Education Academies' (e.g. Gujarat, Kerala and Karnataka) with objectives somewhat similar to the 'Administrative Training Institutes' (ATIs) meant for training the newly recruited officers for Indian Administrative Service (IAS), Indian Police Service (IPS), Indian Forest Services (IFS), Indian Foreign Service (IFS) or State Administrative and State Accounts Services. The trainees of ATIs are the fresh graduates who after passing the competitive examinations of the State or all India level, enter into the administrative, forest, foreign or accounts departments with no prior working experience of the intended job to be assumed. Therefore, the selected candidates require training in specific areas that include inter alia, knowledge of service rules, the Indian Constitution and prevailing administrative rules of the State and so on to shoulder new responsibilities. On the other hand, those recruited for teaching on permanent or tenure positions in colleges/varsities often have some experience of teaching as part time guest faculties and or during their tenure as doctoral/postdoctoral research fellows. Therefore, they get some grooming before occupying teaching positions. Besides, these teachers teach the same subjects that they would have studied during their qualifying degree courses (PG/Ph.D.). Hence, their requirement of training in HRDCs or Higher Education Academies is less crucial compared to those who have to shoulder the administrative responsibilities immediately after graduating. Ideally, courses run by the HRDCs or State Higher Education Academies should help inspire faculty members, improve their teaching skills and research pursuits, and familiarize them with modern pedagogies to make the training meaningful. The benefits of such training programs should percolate down to the learners in colleges and universities. Only then such trainings can be considered relevant and useful.

The OCs/RCs organized by the HRDCs are made mandatory for promotion and increments of teachers. This is the main or compelling reason why teachers participate in such programs. Often, resource persons are chosen from the same university or nearby institutions and they are not necessarily very eminent or inspiring. Further, the resource persons often deliver lectures on the topics of their own choice and not on topics of interest and usefulness to the participants. In any case, the trainees manage to complete the course, collect the certificates and return to their institutions least inspired. They gain little new knowledge that they can utilize in their teaching and research or in inspiring their own students. Unfortunate part is that the UGC did not evaluate the outcome of these programs objectively for too long. At some point of time, a few HRDCs (then called as Academic Staff Colleges) were subjected to assessment by the peer teams of National Assessment and Accreditation Council (NAAC); this author was also part of such teams. However, the exercise was not an outcome-based evaluation. Further, one does not know the impact of these assessment reports. Informal interaction with the trainees of HRDCs generally reveals gloom and disappointment. Many well thought-out steps are essential to revamp the functioning of HRDCs which can make more meaningful contribution towards overall enhancement of higher education scenario in the country especially in the wake of NEP 2020 and herald a new beginning in the field of education. The HRDCs should serve as the premier academic centres for imparting advancements made in a given subject area and current trends worldwide. At the same time, they should also provide information to the trainees on the evolution of education system in India from ancient times to the present (pre- and post-colonial era), clearly convey the meaning and purpose of *higher* education, role of teachers in producing worthy human resource in different fields and need to build self-esteem, pride for the nation, patriotism, and citizenry in the minds of learners. HRDCs need to first define the context, develop the content of their courses, and ensure impactful delivery that is clearly outcome based.

Consequent to globalization and emergence of the three digital waves (internet, internet of things, and now internet of everything—called Third Wave) the new education requirements demand adoption of new pedagogies and use of many digital devices. Also, new focus of education is to promote critical thinking, creative thinking and making innovations. A second most important suggestion of NEP 2020 is integration of diverse borderless subject areas (described in Chapter 4) and reorganization of curriculums. Therefore, HRDCs have to promote propagation of multidisciplinary approach in their training programs. The HRDCs also need to engage in training participants in new teaching pedagogies and use of holistic approach in teaching-learning processes and multidisciplinary approach in research pursuits.

Implementation of NEP 2020 will pose several challenges: administrative, logistic and academic. Therefore, HRDCs can play a decisive role in facilitating smooth implementation of NEP 2020 by sorting out and dealing with the challenges of adopting new pedagogies, integration of various courses, offer of new and need based open electives, skill development and so on through brainstorming sessions, webinars and workshops involving experts with practical experience. Any reformation or adoption of new, creative, and innovative ideas requires great deal of efforts as well as preparing short and long-term vision documents. Major and obvious challenges of HRDCs include (a) diversification of programs, (b) introduction of novel ideas and methodology relating to training and knowledge management, (c) focusing on learner centric approach instead of teacher-centric orientation, (d) modernizing pedagogies of assessment, and (e) developing context-based course contents keeping in mind the needs of the 21st century education and beyond. Invariably execution of new ideas faces resistance; it requires strong conviction, courage and leadership qualities of the head of the institution as well as that of the ultimate regulatory authorities.

The HRDCs also have their own constraints. These include (a) poor or limited administrative support and financial autonomy, (b) insufficient finances and incentives to attract talented resource persons, (c) non-regularization of the services of the HRDC staff as university employees, and (d) lack of enough support from the university system in the development of HRDCs.

Following passages provide some ideas for redesigning course contents of OCs and RCs and their delivery that can enhance the performance and relevance of the HRDCs in the country. The very 'vision and mission' of HRDCs need redefining.

1. Orientation Courses (OCs)

Basic objective of an 'Orientation Course' organized by HRDC is to provide proper direction to the newly recruited faculty members on matters related to the job. For instance, teachers appointed for colleges or universities ought to know the importance of higher education, brief history of education in India from ancient times and, pre-colonial and post-colonial periods, recommendations of various education commissions and committees, impact, merits and demerits of the on-going education system, future needs and so on. The teachers have to be then oriented for the use of modern pedagogies and other required components that are now in vogue globally.

The OC should give practical training on diverse aspects and dimensions of teaching-learning processes. The teachers should also be familiarized thoroughly about the concept of continuous assessment and competency-based assessment procedures like the one advocated by 'Program for International Student Assessment' (PISA) norms. In addition, the OCs should help understand (a) the significance of higher education, which is the pursuit of higher objectives, search for truth, (b) role of teachers in man-making processes, and (c) contribution to skilled and competent men in diverse fields. In the final analysis, higher education is for human resource development and nation building. Such ideas and their significance must be clearly imbued in the minds of trainees. Imbuing the conviction in the minds of teacher participants of OC is that their pivotal role lies in building a humane society, besides training students in chosen fields of studies (e.g. science and technology, medicine, engineering, trade and commerce, foreign affairs, economic growth, literature, philosophy and so on). After all, it is the teachers, who like the sculptors carve statues out of stones: from raw learners to men of high calibre and competency and men of honesty and integrity beset with moral, spiritual, and ethical values. If teachers fail in their task, they also fail the whole nation. Lastly, role of teachers in instilling self-esteem and national pride in the minds of learners needs to be emphasized. In short, to accomplish the above and other goals the purpose of OCs needs to be redefined and the contents redesigned.

2. Refresher Courses (RCs)

'Refresher Courses' (RCs) are supposed to update and refresh the faculty members with regard to the curriculum in vogue and new developments in the chosen fields of studies. Such courses have to be well thought-out and they should depict the current trend of integrating allied and overlapping subjects and also highlight recent advances in the specific fields under discussion. At the same time the pedagogies have to change. At least 50% of the course should be taught by adopting modern pedagogies (see 'Notes'). The participants need training in matters in which they are not thus far very conversant or even familiar. At the end of the training, they should go inspired with new knowledge, newer ways of teaching-learning processes and strong commitment. Only then they can inspire their pupils, teach them how to learn, unlearn and relearn, critical and creative thinking and importance of innovating in the chosen fields/subjects. The RCs should empower the faculty members by imbuing them with new enthusiasm and philosophies of current global trends in teaching-learning-evaluation processes and their significance. Only a competent and inspired teacher can inspire the students.

To sum up, the success of 'Orientation and Refresher Courses' largely rests on two factors: course content and eminence of resource persons. The course content has to be made thematic, modern, dynamic and interactive with an outcome-based objective. It calls for a total redesign of currently operating course contents and pedagogies of HRDCs. Adoption of modern pedagogies and philosophies enshrined in the NEP 2020 are an urgent necessity. As far as resource persons are concerned, only eminent scholars with established academic track record and repute should be chosen. They can greatly inspire and make a long-lasting impact on the minds of participants of RCs.

3. Review of HRDCs

A conspicuously missing component in various academic and research institutions is rigorous review process with respect to various policies and schemes introduced from time to time, outcome of projects, money spent, equipment bought, the outcome and so on. HRDCs are no exception. The benefits of training in HRDCs should reflect improvements in the teaching and research of the trainees, their contribution to curricular developments, adoption of modern pedagogies, inspiring students and so on. Mere collection of feedbacks at the end of a training program is not enough to strengthen the institution of HRDCs in any meaningful way. Collecting and analysing feedbacks from the past trainees should be a continuous process so as to arrive at conclusions objectively. Therefore, mechanisms are needed to enable the participants of OCs/RCs to share their experiences and explain in what way the training was useful and what is the outcome from time to time. Such introspections are essential. Otherwise, training at HRDCs may turn out to be an extravagant activity serving the purpose of fulfilling the requirement of participants for their promotion and increments. The HRDCs should aim at transforming the trainees into competent and committed teachers and researchers. Therefore, an outcome-based periodical review of HRDCs is essential. A dynamic websites for exchange of ideas and feedbacks between the HRDC, participants, and resource persons will go a long way in strengthening the objectives of such training institutions.

4. Other

A linkage between participation in OC/RC with promotion or giving increments is unwarranted. However, certain other incentives like granting duty leave could be considered. Further, some nominal fee should be levied on the participants. If UGC desires to make these courses compulsory then let the participants pay the fees per course (say ₹ 10,000) to cover expenditures at least partially. Having paid for the course, the participants will demand for quality deliberations, better resource persons, books and hand-outs. Also, this may lead to conduct of courses seriously and in a vibrant manner.

The participants of OC/RC should be subjected to continuous evaluation based on seminars, webinars, project works, working in groups, self-learning ability, leadership quality, and creativity. At the end of the courses, examination should be held on the curriculum used for the course by an external agency (online and oral exams) with cut-off marks of say 75% to qualify for receiving the course completion certificates in which marks obtained must be mentioned. Adoption of such practices will familiarize the participants with newer ways of assessment. Simply stated, HRDCs must redesign their OC/RC programs such that the participants learn and master modern pedagogies pertaining to teaching, learning, and evaluation methods practiced worldwide and prepare themselves to apply these parameters on return to their parent institutions. In addition, they should gain new knowledge.

In some States, the State Higher Education Academies are established in recent years. These may also join hands in training the college/university teachers and promote human resource development, as suggested for HRDCs. In addition to training the teachers of government colleges or universities, the State Higher Education Academies may also engage in training teachers belonging to private colleges/varsities. However, this will require suitable modifications in their mandate through cabinet approvals of the respective State Governments. Over a period, such academies of the State could become the sole centres of human resource development with all-inclusive mandates with reference to diverse facets of higher education.

Lastly, the HRDCs should become the partners with universities to bring in change in higher education scenario by resonating with the contemporary compulsions and requirements of reforming higher education systems through practical training. Therefore, the HRDCs across the length and breadth of the country need redesigning the curriculums to accomplish the requirements of the 21st century education on par with the international standards. They can play a supporting role in the smooth implementation of NEP 2020 by preparing teachers who are ready in all respects with reference to their jobs as highlighted earlier in various chapters of this book. After all it is the teachers who have to play a pivotal role in building a strong India that is self-reliant (*Atmanirbhar*), responsive, and prosperous and pave way for humanity, citizenry and national interests to reign supreme.

Chapter 8

Role of State Higher Education Councils

Many transformational rather than mere transactional changes are needed to reform higher education systems in India.

In the past 15 years or so some States of India have established 'State Higher Education Councils' (SHECs) under the aegis of RUSA scheme for quality improvements and regulation of higher education. It is headed by the respective State Ministers of Higher Education as Chairman under whom a Vice Chairman and Executive Director work. The Higher Education Council of each State may have its own need based 'Vision and Mission' avowals. However, generalized and broad-based statements while sounding good do not have much impact on the specific missions to be undertaken in a given time frame of say five years. Therefore, it makes sense to evolve specific mission mode strategies that can be realised within a period of five years and work on them. Each five-year plan should have new and revised missions. It may be emphatically noted that mere transactional interactions with respect to the functioning of universities are not enough unless these usher significant transformational changes. Since the SHECs are apex bodies whose main mission should be to guide and mentor the institutions in their jurisdiction (universities and colleges) to accomplish quality and relevance in higher education. Indeed, quality enhancement in higher education systems is the need of the hour to overcome global challenges and competitions not only in science and technology related developments, economy and employment, but also in managing the international affairs that include trade and business and defence issues. As the world has become a global village, good sustenance of development in any country would depend largely on the quality of higher education. Therefore, the SHECs can do a lot if they are given freedom and headed by visionary educationists (instead of politicians) who have an excellent track record in the field of higher education, vision, concern and commitments. Further, SHECs should be given unstinted administrative and financial supports, freedom and flexibility by the concerned State governments. In the absence of such a support SHECs may not be able to make an impact in transforming the higher education scenario to global standards. Because, any SHEC that is subservient to the State Government, in effect, it will be another State Department working at the behest of the prevailing government machinery.

This chapter highlights how SHECs can play a meaningful role in laying new foundation for quality higher education by evolving appropriate mechanisms of governance and specific game changing directions to universities and colleges for reorganizing the entire education system in response to on-going and perceived global trends and challenges. The Higher Education Councils may evolve policies relevant to twenty-first century needs of the millennial population and in good agreement with the recommendations of the NEP 2020. The new education policy is at best an operating system; it is desirable that the SHECs provide needed software and apps. The on-going massive digital revolution accompanied by the *third wave* of internet, disappearance of many traditional jobs and growing needs of the Gen-Z population with millennial mind set cry for urgent reforms in the education systems to make the learners future ready with acquisition of twenty-first century skills. The Government of India has realized such a need and ushered NEP 2020. The NEP 2020 has identified major defects in the present education system. These include: (a) severe fragmentation of higher educational ecosystem; (b) inadequate importance on the development of cognitive skills and learning outcomes; (c) inflexible disconnection of disciplines, that drives students into narrow areas of specialization without needed domain knowledge; (d) poor standards of UG education; (e) inadequate faculty (both in terms of number and professional competency); (f) lack of institutional autonomy; (g) want of focus on research in universities; and (h) lack of tough and competitive peer-reviewed research funding across disciplines.

The NEP 2020 very rightly emphasizes the urgency of imparting a holistic education by suitable integration of (borderless and closely related) courses and promotion of multi-disciplinary approaches in imparting knowledge at various levels. At the same time it advocates allowing multiple exits and also lateral entries. As per NEP-2020 the first 5 years constitutes the foundational program (Early Childhood Care and Education—ECCE), that is, 3 years of preschool + Grades 1 & 2. The next 3 years (Grades 3-5) are considered as the *preparatory* stage while the subsequent 3 years (Grades 6-8) constitute *middle school*. This is followed by 4 year *secondary stage or high school* (Grades 9-12) in which focus on multidisciplinary study and subject oriented pedagogies providing greater depth, critical thinking, and attention to life aspirations. NEP 2020 lays emphasis on learning how to learn rather than how to master rote-learning.

As far as post Grade-12 education is concerned, the key suggestions of NEP 2020 are (1) universities and colleges to be multidisciplinary in nature, (2) fostering integration of interdependent courses and strengthening integrated approach in teaching and research, (3) providing academic flexibility in choosing subjects (open electives, add-on courses like skill development, etc.), and multiple exit and entry options, (4) mobility from one institution to the other with credit bank facility, and (5) phasing out the affiliating system, and making colleges autonomous. Under the new education policy an UG student can exit with a certificate after completing one year, with a diploma after two years, and with a degree after three years. There is also a four-year degree program with research to enable consolidation of expertise in a chosen subject. A possible and foreseeable consequence of all such options is creation of a huge bureaucracy of certificate production and delivery system. The Master's degree program may consist of one or two years depending upon the UG degree program opted by a candidate. This may create confusion with respect to equivalence across different institutions, different States, and the branch of learning;

it is an anticipatable possibility. Lastly, there is a provision for integrated Bachelor's/Master's degree program with research (five-year course).

A multiplicity of options at various stages can create logistic and operational difficulties to the institutions. For instance, designing integrated degree courses as envisioned by the NEP 2020 is extremely difficult in view of (1) differences in the perception of the academic community itself regarding integration of borderless courses, and (2) multiple exit/entry options. Moreover, learning any subject and mastering it requires the continuity of thoughts and evolution of concepts with progressive increase in complexity. In addition, the institutions need to adopt new teaching pedagogies and tools to make teaching-learning processes learner-centric and at the same time, ensuring global standards. Developing robust, adaptive, accessible, digital teaching-learning platforms for self-learning is the urgent need of the twenty-first century education. Therefore, curriculum development for various courses is a daunting task, and more so for science education. Preparing good curriculums (syllabi) requires great depth and breadth of knowledge in a given subject domain, sub-disciplines and cognate subject areas that have lost sharp boundaries, and competency to judiciously integrate them. The presently existing BOS in most universities with members nominated on the basis of seniority or elected (in some States) may not be in a position to visualize the complexities and prepare course contents of international standards and in accordance with the philosophy of progressive complexities, continuity of thoughts and, proposed multiple exit/entry options. It is indeed a challenging job for subject experts.

Also related to the curriculum is the age-old system of examination/assessment pedagogy that relies on memory-based, textbook-based or content-based boundaries, is no more acceptable when pitted against the global practices. The evaluation system should allow testing the depth of knowledge, competency of learners, ability to self-learn and work in groups and, develop critical thinking and so on. Continuous assessment should more or less replace the semester-end examinations. The protocols for assessment of students of higher classes (UG/

PG) have to be of high standards and enable our students to gain confidence in facing the international challenges when they graduate and leave the college/universities. The perceived challenges of our graduates include procurement of jobs, or undertaking small businesses as entrepreneurs or as start-ups with creative ideas that disrupt existing jobs and create new ones using opportunities offered by the *third wave* of internet.

Higher education normally refers to UG/PG programs that are managed by the universities. Unfortunately, both colleges and universities in vast majority of cases suffer greatly for want of leadership. Furthermore, majority of colleges are run by in-charge principals who are often on the verge of retirement (a consequence of seniority-based assignments!). Likewise universities are run on pro tem basis by appointing senior dean or professor as in-charge or acting Vice Chancellors. Such makeshift arrangements run over several months and even years as the State Governments show little concern or hurry in appointing new Vice Chancellors in time for reasons best known to them. Appointing new Vice Chancellors in advance, before the incumbent person lays down the office is more or less unheard in this country. Most teachers dislike being the officiating principals. Whereas, most teachers in the university take it as a privilege to be in change Vice Chancellors as they see it as a stepping stone for future vice chancellorships and a way of fortifying their CVs. As a rule, such officiating personnel contribute little to the academic growth. In fact, colleges and universities need a leader, a CEO-like academic who means business and has vision, concern and commitment to strengthen both education programs and the institutions.

There also exist numerous other problems with regard to colleges and universities in each State. These pertain to management, recruitment of faculty, transfer of faculty, appointment of governing bodies, UG programs and their contents and so on. Continuous assessment and evaluation of students is more or less absent in traditional universities. All these sectors need reforms to ensure impart of quality education that is relevant to the contemporary needs. Therefore, a good grasp of the multiplicity of complex problems that surround higher education scenario as highlighted above is essential before the

SHECs can attempt to deal, resolve hurdles and inadequacies so as to uplift the higher education to the level that is now needed to withstand global pressures and challenges on one hand and sustaining growth and development of India on the other. It is with this backdrop, what SHECs can do is deliberated below.

Leadership Roles of SHECs

The SHECs should typically play the role of a facilitator rather than of a controller of higher education. The country is now facing many complex intricacies related to the implementation of NEP 2020. It is but natural that reforming higher education, smooth and meaningful implementation of NEP 2020 offers numerous challenges. It is here, the SHECs can play leadership roles in placing the higher education system on a sound footing by eliminating obstacles and facilitating advent of all round reforms in the field of higher education by providing needed guidance, help and academic leadership to institutions that fall in their jurisdiction/province. Illustrative examples of reforms are described below.

(A) Administrative Reforms

Administrative reforms are needed periodically for better governance in all spheres and education institutions are no exception. First, as in the Central Universities, it is desirable to have a Rector or Pro-VC (PVC) in the State universities. The PVC can effectively assist the VC in executing various tasks assigned to her/him expeditiously. Second, the State Universities may also have 'courts' as in the Central Universities. The SHECs could proactively provide for these positions by making suitable amendments in the respective State University Acts.

The apex body of the university concerned with control, regulation and implementation of policies, taking decisions and overall governance is variously called as 'Executive Council', 'Board of Governors', 'Board of Management' or 'Syndicate' as per the University Acts. It is supposed to be a body with clear 'vision and mission' with a mandate to ensure overall development and progression of the institution in a well-planned and transparent manner. However, in reality, most of its time is lost on sanctioning or reconsidering academic or administrative decisions taken earlier. Rarely, time is spent on developing a farsighted long-term vision of the university through a well-planned roadmap and setting time bound goals to accomplish them. It is desirable that such governing bodies, in addition to routine governance play an advisory and visionary role. It should also monitor periodically the progress made under various schemes, and various major divisions of the university (academic, administrative, sports, placement cell, etc.). The SHECs can therefore redefine role of such apex bodies and also evaluate its own performance annually with expert committee ideally consisting of superannuated educationists, bureaucrats, and legal luminaries.

Rules, regulations, procedures, fee structure and admission of students to various courses including doctoral programs differ from one university to the other even in the same State. Likewise, conduct of entrance tests, admission of students to PG courses and research programs, payment of travel allowances, honorariums, provisions of sabbatical and study leaves, and deputation of faculty members to participate in conferences/symposia and so on differ between universities of a given State. Therefore, the SHEC can develop uniform and progressive rules and procedures to be followed across the universities in the State with needed flexibility to universities to allow some differences where needed especially those involving finances (e.g. scholarship to students, daily wagers, salary of guest faculty, etc.).

Second, SHECs may develop strategies to empower universities by facilitating improvement of infrastructure, adoption of ICT in administration, adoption of modern pedagogies in teaching-learning processes, increasing academic flexibility and guide the institutions to acquire global character and image. Following list is an exemplar of possible strategies that SHECs may consider for streamlining and improving the performance of HEIs functioning in their jurisdiction.

1. Improving Governance: Streamlining administration by reducing redundancy, improving responsiveness of administration, accountability, transparency and e-governance;

2. Reorganizing PG Departments into 'Schools' and 'Centres of Advanced Studies' (for greater focus, academic flexibility and autonomy);
3. Smooth integration of allied and borderless areas and development of new courses and curriculums that are context-based, and proper delivery system as envisioned by NEP 2020;
4. Strengthening infrastructure: Departmental and Central facilities;
5. Designing a progressive HR management policy to attract teaching and research talents from India and abroad, and providing attractive career path;
6. Strengthening Human Resource Development Centres (HRDC), University Employment Information and Guidance Bureaus (UEIGB) or Placement Cells;
7. Setting up a Centre for Industry Collaboration (CIC), such linkages can help in providing consultancy, enriching teaching and research, and solving specific problems;
8. Enriching campus life for congenial living and learning;
9. Evolving appropriate strategies for progressive disaffiliation of colleges as per NEP 2020.

(B) Faculty Recruitment

1. SHEC as its top priority should strive to ensure that each college/university has over 90% permanent faculty in place at any given point of time. Most universities are working with <50% of required faculty strength, and manage using unemployed graduates as guest faculty hired on contract.
2. Granting greater autonomy and flexibility to recruit and retain good faculty from across the country: evolving mechanisms to recruit *competent* faculty.
3. Evolving ways for attracting talented persons into the teaching profession at UG/PG levels.
4. Creating rigid rules to avoid *inbreeding* in the appointment of faculty.

5. Making some provision for filling faculty positions by invitation to talented persons from anywhere from India or abroad. Hiring substandard quality teachers will fail to fructify the objectives of NEP 2020.
6. 'Schools' to be set up for greater interaction among academicians, integration and nurture of inter-disciplinary areas and adoption of multidisciplinary approach in research.
7. Training and refreshing faculty on a continuous basis is essential to cope with the new demands of modern pedagogies, use of virtual lecture halls and labs and to reduce *digital gap* between teachers and the learners. This can be accomplished by organizing summer schools by the HRDCs of the university and or the State Higher Education Academies.

(C) Academic Reforms

A hallmark of the twenty-first century is the digital revolution where complex digital systems, AI and the internet revolutions are playing predominant roles. Such technological advances have resulted in the disruption of jobs as discussed elsewhere in the book. Consequently, massive reforms in the academic programs and modernization of infrastructure have become inevitable. The SHECs undoubtedly have the onus of facilitating quality education. A few important suggestions and possibilities in the direction of quality education are listed below.

1. Admission of students to universities may be made on the basis of State Level Entrance Tests. This will provide choice and mobility to students of different regions in the State and promote cross culture hybridization as well creating a vibrant academic ecosystem.
2. Around 25% of the seats could be reserved for students of other states and 15% for overseas students. This will bring in competitive and vibrant academic environment and promote competence and confidence of local students and eventually make them smarter. This will enhance overall learning process. Besides, it is high time to avoid 'frog in the pond' situation.

3. Proper mechanisms may be evolved for sharing resources and faculty between different departments of the university.
4. The BOS may be allowed to have representatives from allied courses, industry and national (research) institutes wherever applicable.
5. Creating 'Flipped Classrooms' and 'Virtual Labs' to incorporate modern pedagogies. For this, high speed uninterrupted internet provision is necessary.
6. SHECs may promote active learning by asking HEIs to incorporate seminars, quizzes, group learning, role plays, project works; creative learning, learning to think, extensive use of ICT, online platforms, MOOCs, various Apps and so on in teaching-learning programs. They may emphasise on teaching 'critical thinking skills' among the faculty and students.
7. Curriculum reforms may be undertaken to ensure: uniform syllabi for mobility and uniformity across the State and to enhance skill development, entrepreneurship and placement, etc. Curriculum should have some parity with the neighbouring States and premier institutions as well (say IISc, IISERs, etc.). This will help reduce issues of equivalence and credit transfers between institutions.

(D) Examination Reforms

Examination reforms are long due. Representative examples are given below:

1. The PG departments may be asked to conduct exams and finalize results. University may then publish the final results.
2. Reforms in setting question papers may be undertaken to ensure commitment of students to gain knowledge. Giving prominence to mere obtaining marks is futile.
3. Creating awareness among the faculty on how to set question papers is very much needed. The question paper should be such that gradation of students becomes takes place on its own. For instance, the question paper

can have a judicious mix of difficult (say 40%), less difficult (30%) and easy (30%) questions.

4. Instead of relying on semester/annual end examinations, it is time SHECs develop a method for continuous assessment thru the course based on the performance of students in semesters, quizzes, project works, group learning, creativity, laboratory works, home assignments, class tests, etc. Competency-based assessment system is needed in place of assessing content-based rote-learning abilities.
5. Each 'School'/Department to have a 'Grievance Redress Cell' as well as, 'Mentoring & Counselling' facilities.

(E) Reforms related to Finance Management

Undertaking resource management is very important for sound financial health of education institutions which are often impoverished due to poor funding. However, there is considerable scope to manage the available funds judiciously, and also build corpus funds for security, stability and for meeting unforeseen needs. Following are some suggestions with respect to finance reforms of the institution.

1. Dormant resources like land and laboratories may be utilized for other useful purposes through PPP model.
2. Human Resources/research capabilities be leveraged for additional projects and programs (e.g. add-on courses) on self-financing mode to generate more funds.
3. Loss making sections whose services are underutilized at present may be shut down and opt for outsourcing (e.g. guesthouse, printing press, workshops, etc.).
4. Services to the stakeholders are made cost effective by proper rationalization of fee structure.
5. Aggressive approach is needed to build up a university corpus with the help of corporates, and donors.
6. All educational institutions have great potential to harness funds through their Alumni Associations for instituting endowments (scholarships, medals, etc.) and improvement of infrastructure facilities.

7. All educational institutions should undergo 'Academic and Administrative Audit' (AAA) each year and record the progress made based on the recommendations of the previous audit. The state councils should have the digital data base of the audit reports and actions taken on them by the concerned institutions.

(F) Promotion of Research

Universities are known globally because of their academic outputs like research, patents, publications and books, awards and recognitions received by the faculty at the national/international levels. Hence, promotion of research in the universities has great many consequences. Following are some suggestions.

1. Encouraging linkages/collaborations with scientists of national laboratories/institutions and arranging their lectures/talks in frontier areas of research.
2. Researchers (students and teachers) may be deputed for study in national/international institutes/laboratories/ industries as and when needed.
3. Providing incentives in the form of research assistants to professors with notable accomplishments and potential for development of technology.
4. Relieving faculty members from administrative works and enabling them to spend more time for teaching and research.
5. Publications in reputed journals to be encouraged.
6. Encouraging teamwork/multidisciplinary research with modern research facilities involving costly equipment.
7. Promotion of research on chosen-specific socio-economic problems of the region (or State) to find implementable solutions.
8. Stringent rules to restrain from plagiarism.
9. Discourage faculty from publishing in predatory journals.
10. Appointment of Research Ombudsman to look into the issues of plagiarism.

(G) Redesigning Women's Universities

Creation of Women's Universities appears to have not made significant impact on the stakeholders, as evident from their overall performance and lacklustre outcomes. The objective of creating such universities cannot be merely for segregating girls from boys. Such universities ought to have notable objectives that are significant and gender specific. Yet, in reality, they deny the opportunity of co-education and its consequent benefits in overall personality development of women. Establishing such universities if absolutely essential, they should have at least one major objective: women's empowerment. Unfortunately, the women's universities offer same courses, already available in the traditional universities. In addition, they have become affiliating universities for Women's colleges in some States (e.g. Karnataka), creating more problems to girl students and their parents staying far off from the location of such universities. The SHECs can help 'Women's Universities' redesign their courses so as to promote empowerment of women more pragmatically. The courses should help students become self-reliant, job ready; instil confidence of entrepreneurship with needed skills and basic knowledge of business/marketing and so on.

Ideally Women's Universities should be residential in nature and not affiliating type. A standalone organization gives better focus needed for its meaningful functioning. Such universities should as a rule have collaboration with industries, Hotels, Tourism and Journalism Departments, Hospitals, Defence Organizations, Police Academies, Agricultural Universities, Engineering and Medical Colleges, Music and Media organizations, Institutions of Performing arts and Fine Arts and so on for strengthening their BOS, Governing Bodies, teaching programs, skill development and so on.

The women's universities should provide unique opportunities by offering courses that interest girl students, and courses not offered in other traditional colleges/universities. Girl students who are purely interested in basic courses (Arts and Humanities, Social Sciences, Sciences, and Commerce etc.) can as well join the traditional universities. Those interested in professional courses (medicine, engineering, agriculture, etc.) anyway join professions colleges and universities offering such courses. It is very much desirable that courses offered in women's universities help girl students not only become empowered and financially independent, but also help nourish their passions. Courses such as: Software Development, AI, Web designing, editing-Photoshop, Computer Aided Designing, Fashion Designing, Interior Decoration, Yoga and Meditation, Nursing and Palliative Care, Physiotherapy, Air Hostess training, Corporate Secretary-ship and Receptionist, BPO, management of Corporate Social Responsibility (CSR), Chartered Accountancy will prove very useful to girl students. The courses on management of Hotels, Catering, Bakery, Food Processing, Hospitals, Home care of patients, Tourism (including home stays), Social work, News Media, Journalism, Beautician Course, Police and Defence Services (except combat), Self Defence and Karate, Horticulture/Floriculture/Bee keeping, Sports & Games including Gymnastics, Swimming, Personality Development, Foreign Languages will also interest the girl students. In addition, training girl students to become 'Teaching Consolers', 'Counsellors & Stress Managers' and Entrepreneurs and so on will go a long way in empowering them; they can seek employments even abroad. Lastly, interested girl students can be trained for positions like the 'Anganwadi Workers'.

The above courses need not be at the graduate or postgraduate degrees only. There can be short-term certificate and diploma courses as well. All it requires is a good grounding and building confidence in the minds of girl students to undertake jobs or venture into starting their own enterprises and thereby provide opportunities of employment to others. Women's empowerment is not just as important as that of men but it is even more important. Therefore, SHECs can play a significant role in realizing women's aspirations.

(H) Bracing with NEP 2020

In the past 3-4 decades many mono-faculty universities have sprouted throughout the country. These include Engineering, Medical, Law and Language (regional languages, Sanskrit Folklore, etc.), Sports and Music. The 'Universities of Agricultural Sciences' gave rise to 'Veterinary', 'Fisheries' and 'Horticulture' universities in certain States. Separate Nursing and Pharmacy Colleges are established which should ideally remain with medical colleges. Such segregation of faculties from the parent universities has certain advantages to the newly set up especially the professional colleges/universities but invariably causes a setback to the parent universities in terms of both academics and fiscal. Furthermore, applied and basic courses should remain together for a closer interaction with each other in teaching and research. Economics, Commerce, and Business Management are no more standalone subjects. These are to be taught together. Besides, these and many other subjects require Mathematics and Statistics too. There are many such examples. Creation of mono-faculty universities is more a political decision than an academic one and also at the cost of tax payer's money. The NEP 2020 advocates for converting mono-faculty universities into multi-faculty institutions.

The set objectives of the NEP 2020 were briefly described earlier in this chapter. For successfully addressing the various issues of concern with respect to higher education, and smooth implementation of the new education policy competent interventions by the SHECs are urgently needed. Leaving implementation aspects to colleges and individual universities can create chaos. Therefore, SHECs have an inexorable role in facilitating realization of the goals enshrined in the NEP 2020.

(I) Annual Review of SHECs

It is a national obligation that every institution is subject to review of their performance periodically. Performance reviews help undertake course-corrections in time before it is too late and, help institutions grow. Therefore, in a democratic country like ours review of the progresses made, innovative changes made in accomplishing smooth functioning of the colleges/ universities and all-round development must be welcomed unhesitatingly and unequivocally. Review should include the functioning of vice chancellors, principals, faculty members and, supporting staff of the colleges and universities using well defined parameters. The tax payers and citizens have a right to know the achievements (besides routine tasks) made by the SHEC, Vice

Chancellors, Registrars, and Executive & Academic Councils and academicians. Success stories and innovative actions of one institution can become model for the other institutions. To accomplish these objectives SHEC may evolve specific mechanisms to review or seek information from each university and publicize it through media and institutional websites. Likewise, it is desirable that review of SHEC's own performance is done by eminent academicians drawn from all India pool of experts in different fields. Academic and Administrative Audits (AAA) of any institution should be done by duly constituted committees whose members do not belong to the given institution. It is best to involve former vice chancellors from the same and/or neighbouring States for AAA of the colleges/varsities/SHECs/ HRDCs and Higher Education Academies etc. The SHECs may actually constitute such committees.

In summary, it is possible for SHECs to undertake many novel reforms related to smooth functioning of colleges and universities of the State. For instance, it can evolve proper guidelines for appointment of vice chancellors and principals, nomination of members to various bodies of the university such as search committee for short listing names for appointment of vice chancellors, executive council, academic council and the senate etc. Similarly, it can evolve uniform and stringent guidelines for awarding honorary degrees, admission of students to various courses and regulations governing various processes, granting study or sabbatical leaves and so on to name a few. SHEC can play the most crucial role in influencing the recruitment of worthy and national/international level faculty and principals and avoidance of inbreeding. If appointment of worthy and competent faculty is in place, everything else will also fall in place. Therefore, SHECs may evolve mechanisms for faculty selection and attraction of talented faculty for both colleges and universities.

The SHEC may proactively undertake several other transactional reforms in educational institutions. For example, it can recommend to concerned State governments to revise the out-dated rules of Transparency Act. A ceiling limit of rupees one Lakh fixed for purchases of scientific equipment, glassware, and chemicals and so on some 30 years ago is inappropriate in present times. The value of rupee has greatly fallen by now. Keeping in mind the inflations, consequent escalations in the price of equipment/procurements, the Act needs upward revision; the higher limit could be raised to say ₹ 10 Lakh.

In all States, there are large number of First Grade Degree Colleges and Universities besides Junior colleges, High schools, Middle schools, and Primary schools. All these institutions have to purchase stationery, books, minor equipment like fans, refrigerators, air conditioners, plastic buckets/containers, cleaning items (soaps, broom sticks, etc.), electric and other items, and many sundry items. As per the prevailing stringent and uninspiring rules, for purchases above certain fixed limit one has to call for multiple quotations, process them and choose the lowest quotation. Such rules are now archaic and unrealistic. The procurement norms should become user friendly-saving, time, energy and undesirable audit observations and harassments, the fears of which prevent many (e.g. a college principal) from procuring essential materials in their terms of office as in-charge or acting officials. Why can't the SHECs promote establishment of government approved shops, the e-portals and Janata Bazars run by Indian companies in all district places and other bigger cities from where institutions can procure their supplies without having to go through the cumbersome and wasteful process of calling for comparative quotations, a mundane task involving time, energy and unexpected audit observations. With such provisions in place, the educational institutions including all government offices can procure their requirements without going through cumbersome processes. This way, most of the administration at the level of the institution can be smoothened by reducing bureaucracy to great extent. The SHECs can thus play a visionary role in the promotion of educational institutions through streamlining and smoothening cumbersome administrative processes. The colonial masters could not trust the natives, and hence created bureaucratic norms, for their own safety. Now in the democratic and republic India we should trust our people, allow them to function smoothly. After all, accountability and freedom go together. However, checks and balances can always be there.

The foregoing passages have highlighted certain issues for overall improvements of higher education system of the country. The SHECs can actually become the agents of change through modernization of education in resonance with various perceivable global challenges and technological advancements. Any lethargy or reluctance to change can be disastrous and even suicidal. The ecosystem of HEIs must improve. These should become magnets of attraction for good faculty to their institutions. Highly talented faculty in a congenial academic environment alone will help usher transformational changes in education and research. Therefore, regulatory bodies like the SHECs, the State Governments, education managers and academicians, should strive (1) to grapple with the changing higher education scenario worldwide, and (2) promote higher education, research and innovation culture in colleges and universities by evolving appropriate strategies to overcome many imminent and pervasive challenges in the process of transformation (e.g. implementation of NEP 2020 in letter and spirit).

Chapter 9

Assessment and Accreditation of Universities: Need for Game Changing Paradigms

Periodic assessment and accreditation of colleges/ universities is necessary to judge their performance, accomplishments, successes and failures, as well as to develop strategies for restitution.

In India, assessment and accreditation of higher education institutions (HEIs), the degree colleges and universities began with the establishment of the National Assessment and Accreditation Council (NAAC) in the year 1994 by the Ministry of Human Resource Development, at Bangalore under the overall control of the University Grants Commission (UGC), New Delhi. Soon thereafter, the NAAC developed methodology for assessment, accreditation and grading the institutions, once in five years. Initially, very few institutions opted for undergoing the accreditation process possibly due to certain apprehensions and fears. However, with time many institutions fell in line and opted for assessment and accreditation by the NAAC. Yet, not all HEIs of the country are accredited as of now due to sheer vastness of the numbers (more than 911 universities and 41,900 colleges). Yet it is a fact that assessment and accreditation process has been a worthwhile exercise and beneficial to the institutions as it has led to their improvements in the course of time. The improvements generally include, face-lifting of the buildings, campus maintenance, embellishment of physical infrastructure that include addition of classrooms, computer and language labs, renovation of certain campus amenities, ICT facilities, and subscription to research journals to name a few. The institutions desirous of accreditation also quickly registered Alumni Associations (often just prior to the visit of the Peer Team), signed a few MOUs with industries or other institutions and so on. By and large, improvements in the physical infrastructure are the major impacts of NAAC. But, what impact all this has on enhancement of quality in education (e.g. making learners future ready) is yet to be assessed.

The assessment methodology has undergone changes periodically. Likewise, grading the institutions has undergone changes from 5-stars to the present seven-point scale i.e., 'A++' to 'C' grade. Such changes are effected based on the inputs of the peer team committee members, institutions and wisdom of the accrediting agency to ensure improvements by ironing out certain difficulties encountered in grading. Yet, the basic philosophy has largely remained the same. There are seven main criteria used in the assessment and accreditation of the universities. These are as follows:

1. Curricular Aspects
2. Teaching-Learning and Evaluation
3. Research, Innovation and Extension
4. Infrastructure and Learning Resources
5. Student Support and Progression
6. Governance, Leadership and Management
7. Institutional Values and Best Practices

The colleges and universities should align themselves for assessment and accreditation of their institutions according to the new methodology namely 'Revised Accreditation Framework' (RAF) effective from July 2017. As per the new methodology, the institutional inputs are received online and assessed separately, and not by the peer teams. There has been a paradigm shift from qualitative peer judgment to data-based quantitative indicators, with increased objectivity and transparency following the use of ICT, confirming scalability and robustness. The pre-qualifier now is 25% of System Generated Score. Out of the total number of metrics, about 70% of them come under Quantitative Metrics (QnM) and 30% under Qualitative Metrics (QlM). The data validation is done by the third party. The abbreviated peer team visits are essentially meant to verify the claims of the institution. This ensures a greater transparency on the part of NAAC and, accountability on the part of the institutions desirous of assessment and accreditation. Yet, no method is fool proof. In the new methodology also certain lacunae may still exist.

In addition to NAAC that accredits conventional colleges and universities, the 'National Board of Accreditation' (NBA) established by AICTE (1994) and the 'National Institutional Ranking Framework' (NIRF) established by the Ministry of Education (MOE) in 2015 are involved in accreditation of institutions imparting technical/professional education like the Engineering, Management, Pharmacy, Law, Medical, Architecture, Dental and Research. The NBA is a part of Washington Accord since 2014. Institutions falling under the purview of NBA/NIRF may refer to the respective websites for details pertaining to assessment criteria, weightage points and so on.

For an accrediting agency, evolution of new and need based criteria of assessment from time to time are a continuous process. Nevertheless, assessment processes must make an impact on the quality and credibility of HEIs, lest the whole exercise turns out to be futile. Furthermore, the accrediting agencies should strive to become the agents of change in the higher education systems, modernizing them to stay relevant, and cater to the pressing needs of the on-going and anticipating developments of the future especially those arising due to the digital revolutions. The expediency lies in the fact that the new industrial revolution (IR 4.0) characterized by the complex digitization necessitates acquiring new skills to meet the challenges of the technology driven disruption in jobs chiefly in the wake of the *third wave* of internet revolution. Today, HEIs are required to provide education to prepare learners who can readily and effectively face challenges of globalization by acquiring twenty-first century skills. The entire education system is poised to undergo metamorphosis by adopting modern pedagogies of teaching-learning-assessment processes, embracing multidisciplinary approach to the study of a given subject to develop higher competency. The examination system is poised to change from assessing students on the basis of content-based rote-learning to competency development. Continuous assessments based on performances in seminars, quizzes, execution of projects, group learning, self-learning and ability to innovate are needed. All this calls for novel paradigms of education and assessment in future years. Therefore, the accrediting agencies can and should serve as the agents of change in the higher education by adopting outcome-based assessment and accreditation of higher education institutions.

A principal agency like the NAAC which has undertaken assessment and accreditation of universities and colleges in the past 25 years has accumulated vast experience and data, for analysis. Hence, it is in a position to revisit and analyse the data to cull out information on the impact of each criterion it has used in grading the institutions. A revisiting is necessary to know what impact the present parameters (e.g. feedback of students on syllabi, ICT based teaching and learning, linkage with industries, placements, alumni association, etc.) have actually made on the quality enhancement of teaching and learning processes and institutions. Another equally important issue is how do we evaluate the various kinds of claims made by the institutions? How to take cognizance of negative and often disturbing issues such as large number of copying cases, plagiarism in research, publications in predatory journals, repetitive research outputs, incidences of harassments to girl students, court cases filed by the employees on the management (indicators of injustices or wrong decisions taken by the administration with reference to service matters) and so on? Further, in any HEI, teaching activity must take the centre stage. Yet, in many colleges/varsities the number of permanent faculty members on the roll is 50% or less than the sanctioned number. Therefore, major teaching work is carried out by the contractual faculty. Still the institutions get high ranking by the NAAC possibly because of the little importance given to faculty strength in the parameters used for accreditation. Likewise, inadequacy of facilities for girl students whose number often exceeds or equals that of the boys in most HEIs is a matter of great concern that demands giving adequate attention to providing needed amenities to them. Poor facilities for girl students are sure to discourage them from going for higher education. This is more serious than most of us would like to believe. Therefore, accrediting agencies should evolve separate parameters to judge the adequacies of facilities provided to the girl students. Given better facilities enrolment ratio girls might very well increase significantly.

Clearly, there is a need to identify novel parameters to judge the quality in teaching, learning, and assessment processes. At the same time, we need to do away with the out-dated criteria that do not serve the desired purpose. The new parameters may replace those that have now become irrelevant or redundant. Now more than ever, new parameters to help judge the quality of 'content delivery' and outcomes of learning processes need to be in place. Also, following implementation of NEP 2020 the accrediting agencies may have to evolve novel parameters to assess the outcome of the new education policy in letter and spirit. Evolving such parameters is by no means easy; it is in fact quite challenging.

Let us also raise a few questions. Should the parameters of assessment be the same for first time and subsequent times (reaccreditations) or they have to differ? Should the parameters and methodology used in reaccreditation not encompass *hope of rising and fear of falling* (getting higher or even lower scores)? We may also debate on whether reaccreditation is indeed necessary. If yes, at what interval and why? To some extent clarification is provided in the NAAC manuals but debate and discussion on such issues are very much warranted.

Clearly, the accreditation agencies have an opportunity to serve as agents of change in higher education; therefore they can subtly energize the institutions to enhance the quality of higher education in the country by developing new parameters of judgment that are quantifiable and unambiguous in nature. The new parameters have to be relevant to the contemporary needs and changing scenario of higher education impacted by the inescapable influence of the industrial/digital revolutions, disruption in jobs, need to create new jobs that require new skills, readiness to deal with many unforeseen situations like the pandemics, disasters like the earthquake, landslide or deluge and so on.

After creating the basic infrastructure, the two major areas that determine the performance of HEIs are (1) quality of faculty in adequate numbers, and (2) good governance with leadership. If so, future accreditation and assessment parameters should be such that they focus on revealing the actual status and outcome in these two areas. Adoption of an outcome-based assessment is likely to motivate institutions to improve quality of education. Following passages highlight certain specific issues in response to which new parameters may be evolved by the assessment and accreditation agencies.

The first and foremost issue pertains to quality of academic programs, and having competent faculty in place. This is important because, impart of quality education, creation of new knowledge, preparation of study materials, making innovations in pedagogies, modernizing teaching-learning-evaluation processes depend solely on the competency of the academicians, the teaching faculty. Hence, assessment parameters need to lay emphasis on (1) recruitment of required numbers of faculty members, (2) competency of teachers recruited and quality of teaching, (3) adoption of modern pedagogies, and (4) the outcome. Often, faculty strength in colleges and universities is found way below the required numbers; this includes top graded universities too. In recent decades, bulk of teaching work is shared by the locally available unemployed graduates appointed on contract basis. This has led to shoddy and substandard educational quality. Interestingly, often the members of the peer team themselves argue that State Governments do not allow filling up of vacancies, so it is not the fault of the institution and therefore they need not be given lower grades. This sympathetic approach can be self-defeating. Giving an 'A' Grade to institutions where the permanent faculty strength is less than 80% of the sanctioned strength can at best serve as an incentive for not appointing permanent faculty. As if this is not enough, most colleges (including the constituent colleges) are run with *ad hoc* principals and, universities with *ad hoc* vice chancellors for months and years as the concerned State/Central Governments do not promptly fill up the vacancies. Depriving institutions of effective leadership is a sure way of ensuring stunted growth and sustenance of education. Therefore, the accrediting agencies should fix parameters of assessment that necessitate filling all teaching positions as well as appointing heads of the institutions without any delay. It is an academic issue and not a political one. So why hesitate in imposing stringent norms to appoint required numbers of faculty members in the interest of the nation? Such assertions by the assessment agencies will force the State/Central governments to fall in line and care for higher education to ensure welfare of the State and the nation. It is time to realize that running education systems largely with contractual faculty will not usher reforms. Besides, it is obvious that the education system will not be the same post-Covid-19. In the absence of adequate number of competent faculty, the implementation of NEP 2020 will also suffer greatly as it will be impossible to adopt new pedagogies. Therefore, accrediting agencies like the NAAC should evolve many new parameters ('criteria' and 'key aspects') of Assessment and Accreditation of HEIs in the foreseeable future.

Good governance of HEIs is one most important issue. Rise and fall of any institution greatly depend upon the leadership and governance that play a pivotal role in building institutions of repute (Chapter 2 this book; and Saidapur 2019b). So, if HEIs desire to progress rapidly, Principals and Vice Chancellors (s the case may be) have to toil hard to provide both quality governance and leadership. Therefore, their performance using appropriate criteria points and key aspects should become an important aspect in grading the institutions. Such parameters will force them to be more accountable and proactive. Assessment of the heads of the institutions should be with respect to their actual contribution towards academic, administrative, finance related reforms and new initiatives taken, if any, during their tenure in office, and, transactional as well as transformational changes effected if any. Again, all this requires use of novel parameters. In future, performance of vice chancellors also needs to be assessed using parameters that reflect implementation of NEP 2020, creating modern infrastructure for online, and offline education, facilitating adoption of modern pedagogies and so on. In short, it calls for formulating new incisive parameters to assess and grade the governance and leadership of the institutional heads. Often the peer team members are considerate and give liberal grades for governance by the head of the institution. I know a university where the peer team gave high scores for governance and a few days later the vice chancellor was suspended by the chancellor and subjected him to judicial enquiry! This should not happen as it can undermine the credibility of accrediting agency.

In parallel with the changes in the teaching-learning pedagogies, there is a need to adopt new methods for assessment of students. The assessment methods have to be of global nature and standards. The new assessment methods have to focus on competency based continuous assessment using well-designed protocols. These may include judging student's performance in seminars, quizzes, home assignments, project works, group learning, and ability to work with others, creative thinking and innovating. Therefore, parameters of accrediting agencies will have to include aspects related to (continuous) assessment of students and methods practiced in the institution under grading.

It is desirable that the HEIs have firm and stringent mechanisms to discourage copying in examinations, plagiarism in research, sexual harassments, corruption and fraudulent practices in the utilization of funds and so on. Accordingly, assessment agencies should take cognizance of these aspects by developing relevant parameters. There can be some grade points for generation of fiscal resources by the institution. All these determine the quality of governance and should come under assessment and accreditation processes as novel parameters.

In recent decades, the number of girl students has been steadily exceeding that of the boys in colleges as well as in universities. Further, good number of women faculty is engaged in teaching in the universities. Therefore, the institution must be sensitive to the needs of girl students and women faculty. Ideas for creating good ambience and facilities for girl students of degree colleges were recently described (Saidapur 2019c). The same applies for universities. The assessing agency may consider evolving a few specific key aspects and parameters to assess adequacy of such facilities. This will go a long way in promoting the cause of women's education and enhancing their enrolment ratio in higher education institutions.

To sum up, higher education is poised for restructuring in the light of global compulsions and implementation of NEP 2020. In accordance with the envisaged changes, there arises a need for new parameters of assessment of HEIs. The suggestions made in the forgoing passages are merely representative in nature. After a thorough discussion, the methodology of assessment and accreditation of institutions can be refined to include novel parameters. From time-to-time new parameters have to be evolved that meet contemporary requirements. The great philosopher Socrates opined that *the unexamined life is not worth living*. In a similar vein, policies unexamined are not worth their existence.

Now more than ever, HEIs have to be assessed chiefly keeping in mind the learning outcomes and their relevance to global challenges. Therefore, HEIs are obliged to usher unfeigned transformational changes to enable meeting the national and global challenges, as well as the unforeseen challenges like the spread of Covid-19, calamities and so on. Thus, in the swiftly changing global scenario, numerous technology driven disruptions in jobs, pandemics and other calamities, the entire education system needs revamping, rejuvenation and total metamorphosis. This is the context and it should influence the content and the assessment parameters. Therefore, it is highly desirable that the accrediting agencies strive to become the agents of change; that is making higher education relevant, by espousing insistent parameters of assessment and accreditation.

Chapter 10

Reflections on the Future of Higher Education and Universities

Every university has its problems. The issues range from lack of amenities, plagiarism, poor quality research, sexual harassment, faculty moonlighting, and faulty and biased recruitment.

—Sanjaya Baru

The universities of the twenty-first century are under enormous pressure for performance in the face of issues arising out of rapid advances in science and technology, emergence of digital revolutions, globalization, and undeniable impact of all these on education. The universities largely suffer from (1) poor leadership and governance, (2) a lack of adequate number of competent faculty, (3) obsolete curriculum, and (4) financial crunches and political interferences. These have pushed our universities to a morass situation. The universities need resurrection and remodeling if they have to meet the challenges of the twenty-first century. Worldwide, credibility and credentials of universities have increased, and many countries have become very successful in attracting students and talents from all over the world. On the other hand, in India, barring a few premier institutions, most others produce substandard and unemployable graduates. Highly meritorious graduates emerging out of premier institutions generally prefer to migrate to developed countries of Europe, or America and Australia. Not many bright candidates desire to join the State varsities as faculty. The State varsities that lack vibrant academic ecosystem are forced to continue the *business as usual* with the inbred and often unworthy faculty. Historically, many factors (like nepotism, favouritism, corruption, reservation, etc.) have contributed to driving away the talent from the education systems. This is in a way self-destructive, self-inflicting and self-reinforcing behaviour on the part of HEIs.

Even the mobility of UG/PG students (non-professional courses) is generally restricted to colleges affiliated to the same university due to restrictions, the varsity policies. Such policies are not conducive for quality teaching-learning processes, as the students miss a competitive environment. Therefore, it is necessary to assuage aspirations of students to study in any of the State universities/colleges, subject to fulfilling prescribed eligibility criteria (e.g. Entrance Test scores) as done for professional courses.

Today, most universities suffer from a visible absence of worthy leadership and governance. Appointment of unworthy professors as vice chancellors is the principal reason for downfall of universities on all fronts; imperfect soldiers made 'Generals' can hardly win the battle leave alone the wars. A mediocre vice chancellor fails to provide academic leadership and quality governance and eventually derails the university and pushes it to oblivion. A corrupt vice chancellor will spread corruption throughout the university system in no time making it difficult to undo the corruption culture. Today more than ever we need vice chancellors of high honesty, integrity and competency. Such people are definitely available to head the varsities, it is just that they are not politically connected and also do not go around lobbying to secure the coveted position. Furthermore, the governments in power show little urgency in appointing vice chancellors on time leaving the universities to fend for themselves with ad-hoc arrangements for several months and sometimes for years.

Another crucial component is the faculty recruitment. Appointing a mediocre faculty ensures damage to several generations of students. The faulty appointment processes are guided by nepotism, favouritism, corruption, reservation, and mercy promotions. Secondly, most teaching programs are run by contractual faculty who are often the local unemployed graduates. However, great universities are built by the hard work of eminent faculty who practice building the culture of academic excellence, make innovations and indulge in producing trained man power (human resource) imbued with moral and ethical values. It is this eminent faculty which brings name and visibility to the universities.

Undeniably, neglect of education sector has led to long-term damage of the country. University education is supposed to address seen and unseen challenges and make human life comfortable and meaningful. A point of great relevance to higher education is the fact that the twenty-first century will prove to be the most challenging one in human history. Technological advances especially the digital revolutions and use of AI and machine learning have surpassed all human imaginations and their impact is unparalleled. The managers of HEIs have to quickly grasp the prevailing and foreseeable exigencies and reshape all universities of the country. With these trepidations in mind some major reflections of concern are portrayed below.

Reflection 1

Education scenario is fast changing globally with the advent of *third wave* of internet, AI, and easily available MOOCs. Undeniably, the universities are under great pressure for reshaping and repurposing their 'vision and mission'. Perceptibly, primary aim of universities is providing education in various disciplines and sub-disciplines of interest. Ultimate aim is human resource development. Together, they facilitate advancements in science and technology, agriculture, medicine, liberal arts, fine arts and numerous other areas including protection of environment and strengthening international relationships to name a few. As a matter of fact everything related to welfare of the nation exclusively depends upon the quality and competency of graduates emerging out of the universities. In a highly competitive world highly advanced and endowed nations design strategies for domination over the others. Hence, India needs to be sensitive to such consequences, and accordingly design her varsity education that clearly depicts far-reaching consequences.

Reflection 2

The universities can no longer go on with *business as usual* by simply awarding myriad of certificates and degrees without quality assurance and brand name that prospective employers wish to see in job seekers. Looking beyond, people now look for global citizenship following technological advancements like the 'internet of everything'. The *first wave* (1985-99) with the building of internet heralded the 'online' world. It also ushered many technology-related developments. In the field of education it contributed to both technology and online courses (e.g. use of power points, videos, simulations, content sharing, and platforms of MOOCs etc.). The *second wave* of internet (2000-2015) resulted in the popularly known 'internet of things' (IoT). It is driven by platforms like the Google, Facebook, Twitter, Amazon and so on leading to 'App-based Economy' and 'Mobile Revolution' (e.g. Search, Social & Commerce, and Start-ups on top of the internet) which essentially closed the dial up businesses. The ubiquitous connectivity, a hallmark of the *third wave* (since 2016), the 'internet of everything', has allowed the entrepreneurs to transform major real-world sectors including education sector at all levels. Therefore, the transformative value of the third wave must become a component of education as it offers an extraordinary opportunity and, at the same time, an existential threat if not utilized fully.

Reflection 3

The advances in the third wave and AI are both technology-driven and App-driven and have great impact on various spheres of human activities as well as on education itself. The future education is set to rely heavily on 'online' and use of online platforms. These have advantages as well as limitations. Online education should not end the face-to-face teaching-learning processes merely to save on expenditures. Besides, online education is not a substitute to active learning but it is necessary and supplementary. The Covid-19 pandemic has enhanced the utility of online education transiently, or may be even permanently. In any case, role of teachers is set to change from, *sage on the stage to guide on the side*. A teacher's role will be more of a mentor, facilitator, guide, philosopher, and friend. To assume such roles, teachers need preparation, training and orientation. Future teachers will need reorientation not only towards digital pedagogies but also learn newer ways of teaching (e.g. creative thinking, problem solving, innovating, etc.) and continuously strive to overcome the *digital divide* between them and the learners. Predictably, learners are more likely to be ahead of their teachers in the use of digital devices and apps.

Reflection 4

In the fast changing global scenario, the universities need to establish partnerships with stakeholders, industries and other premier institutions in India and abroad for tackling national/ global problems. They must engage in addressing local issues as well as knowledge transfer on various issues including health and hygiene. For example, traditional universities in the country which have PG departments of microbiology, biotechnology, and biochemistry can actively work for developing technologies like vaccine production, diagnostic tools and laboratories, on their own or in collaboration with industries or start up entrepreneurs. Likewise, the department of Chemistry and Computer Science can develop methods of reducing steps in producing pharmaceuticals and drug designing in collaboration with industries for commercial production or transfer of technology. If each university produces one vaccine or one commercially useful compound or one pharmaceutical compound, it will amount to thousands of such products for the country. Any success in this direction will greatly boost the country's economy. Additional benefit is training students and instilling confidence in them to join industries or undertake start-ups. In the long run universities will have a large network of such entrepreneurs, industries and start-up business establishments for mutual benefits. Clearly, linkage between universities and industries (especially the start-ups) will pave way for national growth and sustenance. Even university faculty, the 'Professors of Practice' may be given sabbatical leave with substantial grants (or loan) to undertake start-ups in their chosen fields. This will also generate enormous confidence in the minds of learners. In short, anything the universities can do to enliven lives of citizens will matter.

Reflection 5

Curriculum development and delivery of contents are the two important aspects of higher education (see Chapter 4). The course content should be evolved in relation to the context and it should be outcome based. Therefore, those involved in preparing the curriculum ought to first define the context. Second, each discipline has grown in its scope and dimension due to generation of new information continuously from the related or cognate areas. Besides, a deeper understanding of a subject is required to appreciate multidisciplinary approach particularly in research. Therefore, integration of borderless subjects in teaching-learning processes and research is inevitable now. Such an approach will go a long way in breaking down the silos and establish more useful partnerships within the institution and outside of it. However, metamorphosis of existing curriculums into totally transformed new courses with integration of borderless domains is not easy. Eminent experts with sound holistic knowledge of the given discipline are needed for properly integrating closely related subject areas and evolve new courses. A good curriculum is an operating system and directive in nature.

The second dimension pertains to delivery of curriculum by the faculty. Ideally, a course should be taught by a single teacher so that teaching can go on sequentially and in a methodical way. The teacher should also have freedom to upgrade curriculum in light of new developments from time to time (academic flexibility). Teachers need to be encouraged to prepare course notes, books, manuals for practical courses, plans for field works and projects, develop group-learning strategies, problem-solving practices, use of various Apps and so on. Faculty members may desirably undertake researches to tackle local, national or global problems and find solutions.

Reflection 6

The policies of recruiting faculty members and appointing vice chancellors for universities need to be transparent and purely competency based. The appointees at the higher level in the ladder must have national and international stature. They may be from any part of India or abroad. Merit, competency, commitment, honesty and integrity should constitute the prime choices in such appointments if we have to build universities with excellence and global standards. Inbreeding and recruitment of mediocre faculty have greatly diminished the credibility of our universities. Countries attain pinnacles of successes due to the hard work of talented youth, committed and competent people. There is no dearth of talent or talented people in India. It is time to realize the importance of attracting globally competent people (non-resident Indians as well as foreign nationals) to our country to work as teachers, researchers, entrepreneurs and so on. This is how the western world has grown. Driving the talent away from the universities is an unforgivable sin. India can no longer remain complacent letting the brain-drain flourish and light the lamp of Europe, America, Australia or other developing and developed countries, and she herself remain in dim light. With appropriate policies in place, India can show its potential of crafting universities like the Oxford, Cambridge, Harvard, Yale or Stanford in the near or distant future. Unambiguously, this surely calls for a change in the political will guided by a long-term vision and support.

Reflection 7

The regulatory bodies which oversee the working of universities also need reforms. In response to changing global scenario they must shun the colonial mind set of 'controlling' for uniformity and this has eroded the autonomy of universities. Instead, they should strive to provide visionary leadership with futuristic ideas and facilitate building a culture of excellence in universities. They should encourage universities to undertake specific studies/researches for tackling local, national, or global issues, and promote cross culture hybridization of faculty and students and creating vibrant academic environment.

Often schemes of regulatory bodies have built in flaws. For instance, intermittent insistence on NET qualifications followed by exemptions, introduction of 'Faculty Improvement Program' (FIP), 'Merit Promotion Scheme', 'API assessment protocol for recruitment and promotion of faculty', and the 'BSR professorship scheme' are some examples which effectively diluted academic standards in the universities. Likewise, insistence on publication of two research papers before submission of doctoral theses gleefully promoted overnight mushrooming and registration of thousands of predatory journals with dubious distinction, as commercial enterprises and have been flourishing thanks to the policies of regulatory bodies, and to the detriment of academic growth of universities.

A classic example is the UGC's BSR Faculty Fellowship Scheme. It offers fellowship to superannuated science teachers of universities who have successfully guided fifteen doctoral students; this is no measure of competency, eminence or merit. If one can supervise 5 or 10 students, is it difficult to supervise a few more to reach the magic number 15? It is more of a cloning business. As a matter of fact, good academicians do not attribute much importance to numbers be it publication of research papers or guiding students for their doctoral degrees. An unfortunate consequence is that the scheme has successfully excluded many distinguished highly recognized faculty members, fellows of premier science academies and recipients of prestigious awards like the Shanti Swarup Bhatnagar Prize for not supervising 15 doctoral dissertations. Such schemes incentivize repetitive researches of no consequence, at the expense of tax-payers' money. Ideally, research and teaching interests should not compete with each other. In universities, overemphasizing engagement on research adversely affects teaching and training the graduate students.

The various flawed policies cited above as examples deserve scraping at once. The various regulatory bodies that oversee the governance of universities must strive to bring about transformational rather than transactional changes in higher education. In brief, the regulatory bodies of 21st century should change their mandate from 'regulation and control' to 'facilitation and guidance'.

Reflection 8

We need to build universities with high credentials and credibility, create brands that prominent business establishments would value and gainfully employ the graduates coming out of our universities. Today, universities are suffering from existential crisis as their certifications (certificates/diplomas/degrees) are steadily losing credibility. The IITs, IISc, and IISERs and few other premier institutions are exceptions. The moot question is can India become an innovative and entrepreneurial hub nation without becoming a centre of attraction to the global best and the brightest? Indian universities need to rise to a level that can attract global talents for teaching, research collaborations, and also for start-up and entrepreneurial undertakings conjointly. Indian Government, the various State Governments, education managers, the intelligentsia must think seriously to make up their mind to pave way for reshaping and repurposing the universities. For this political will is essential as hard decisions have to be taken, implemented and supported.

Reflection 9

In the past, India has addressed the issues like 'right to education', 'access, equity and excellence'. We now need to move from these objectives to 'right education' and 'right way of education'. The current century demands education in creative and critical thinking, innovating and, skill development. Accordingly, these are now the integral components of new education system. Furthermore, in the context of the twenty-first century, uneducated people are not those who cannot read or write but those who fail to *learn, unlearn,* and *relearn* (Alvin Toffler). Universities need to facilitate self-learning. Online education is not the ultimate solution. A judicious blend of offline and online education is needed keeping in mind the constraints of reaching the rural and urban poor in mind as well as the availability of high speed internet facilities and digital devices for all.

Reflection 10

A major tenet of future education revolves around redesigning and repurposing of higher education to accomplish desired results. Focus needs to be on acquisition of entrepreneurial skills, learning to do and developing and sustaining innovation culture (generating value for research). The NEP 2020 is a step forward, and a great opportunity of remodeling our higher education. It must be implemented in letter and spirit. In the past, various education commissions were set up and reports were sought (Thyagarajan, 2019). However, recommendations of these reports were only partially implemented. Hopefully, the same fate will not befall on the NEP 2020 despite many challenges such as: evolving context-based curriculums for various courses, ensuring proper content delivery mechanisms, adopting modern pedagogies, orienting and training the teachers, dealing with numerous exit/entry options and so on. Guarding the credibility of myriads of certificates issued to students after each year of their studies in UG/PG education is a challenge of consequence because it is necessary to ensure their utility values and overcoming problems of equivalence of certificates across the institutions and so on.

Reflection 11

The universities are facing existential crisis, but most academicians and political masters refuse to foresee. In this highly competitive era, higher education systems need total remodeling. Therefore, the universities need autonomy and freedom to reshape and repurpose higher education. The regulatory bodies should become advisory bodies. They should strive to provide leadership, wisdom, and timely inputs on the futuristic and global trends and allow the universities to respond in their own ways. With low investments and lack of autonomy the universities are unlikely to reach the global standards. Sanjaya Baru, the author of *Accidental Prime Minister* remarked, "Every university has its problems. The issues range from lack of amenities, plagiarism, poor quality research, sexual harassment, faculty moonlighting, and faulty and biased recruitment" (*Source*: Google). The statement of Mr. Baru aptly summarizes the prevailing plight of the universities and, it is a loud wakeup call as well.

Inadequacy and poor performance of public funded HEIs, has resulted in the emergence of large numbers of private institutions (colleges and universities) all over the country. These are generally expensive in nature and mostly the rich or well-to-do people can study there. Professional education (e.g. engineering and medicine) is almost out of reach of the poor. It is a cause for concern. Secondly, the country is endowed with enormous demographic dividend in the form of youth population. Therefore, it is necessary that youth energy is channelized and motivated with quality education. Denial of educational opportunities can transform this demographic dividend into 'demographic liability' or even 'demographic catastrophe'. Dismissing such a possibility as mere conjecture can prove costly. Undeniably, futuristic strategies are needed to avoid such situations in the near or distant future. Moreover, with passage of time, the current demographic dividend of youth population will without doubt transform into an aged population. What are the country's foresights and preparations to meet such a situation? Numerous issues have already arisen for senior citizens following nuclear form of families. The universities have also to resonate with all such problems of the society by remodeling their mandates.

Reflection 12

The declining standards and inadequacy of higher education in public funded institutions has provided space for private organizations to start colleges, and universities. They may provide better infrastructure, good faculty, and attract good students. Such institutions mostly offer technical/professional courses for the well to do people. The prevalence of foreign universities may someday affect even the premier institutions like the IITs, IIMs, IISc and so on. So what should we do? The country must face the challenge by equipping our own HEIs with better infrastructure, excellent faculty, autonomy, generous financial support and so on. In addition, allow them to establish partnership with premier institutions functioning in India and abroad, through twining programs and strike a balance between Indian culture/ethos and technical advancements.

Reflection 13

An important aspect of higher education is to produce human resource that is present and future ready. It is surely a tricky issue. Job-ready degrees are not a substitute for tertiary education or higher education. Narrow specializations do not bestow competency, skills to handle diverse and, unforeseen challenges. Therefore, a good grounding in fundamentals, developing competency with confidence is essential. Further, future jobs may all be temporary in nature. Also, in future times, it will be very difficult to predict the nature of future jobs. While remodeling the higher education, these constraints have to be considered rather seriously. Yet, new concerns may arise from time to time. For instance, some people now think that higher education may itself require disruptions. Who knows, in future, the private companies may come forward and provide training (education) to post Grade-12 students and absorb them in their industries? Seemingly, naïve and out of box ideas like these may someday become the reality. Who can predict the future anyway?

Closing words: To sum up, the universities must now strive unfailingly to do everything possible for transforming the society: bridging the gaps and divides (urban-rural, digital, economic, and social) between people, channelizing youth energy for nation building and preparing for global citizenship. At the same time, higher education should help in shaping social behaviour, inculcation of moral and ethical values, importance of honesty and integrity, national pride, patriotism, and citizenry. Not all citizens of this great nation are equal in every respect: wealth, prosperity and education. It is impossible to make everyone equal with respect to everything. Therefore, divides originate between the inhabitants of any country; education should help reduce such gaps. Thanks to technological advancements, the mobile phones that have reached all levels of the society including the rural mass living in villages, the young generation is picking up the use of mobile technology very fast. However, provision and access for high speed internet facility will haunt for quite some time and incapacitate online education, businesses, entrepreneurial undertakings, and the poor (rural/urban). Universities need to address all such issues to make life of citizens and netizens enliven. For this to happen, universities need academic freedom, well-defined purpose and commitment, first-rate faculty, and generous financial support and total freedom from political interferences. Only then we can fix accountability on universities with respect to their performance and contribution as they are supported by the public money. It is worth noting that the rich and well to do people or those who can afford, are opting for higher education in foreign countries because they expect better education and certificates that carry brand names and assure their upcoming life. Let us look at the amount spent annually by the Indian students for study abroad in the past three years: US $1875.8 billion in 2019, $1156.6 billion in 2020 and $1965.4 in 2021 under the 'Liberalized Remittance Scheme' (LRS) introduced in 2004 (*The Indian Express of October 21, 2021, Google*). Nearly 20 billion US dollars are remitted for study abroad and, some 24 billion dollars for travel since 2014. Furthermore, footprints of foreign universities are poised to increase in the near future, which may take away good teachers and researchers as well as bright students from the traditional universities. This may have an intimidating effect on the future prospects of our universities. Therefore, the importance of remodeling the Indian universities to reach global standards does not need further emphasis. Clearly, our universities can no longer go on with *business as usual*. But are we doing exactly that?

Postscript

This book is an outcome of my inner urge to share my deep concerns and perceptions on the need for resurrection of higher education in India. This is unavoidable and urgent. India must gear up quickly to meet the on-going and future challenges of the twenty-first century especially the digital revolution that has not only caused irreversible job disruptions but also threatening nations to condemn to slavery of a different kind, colonization by companies. Such a threat is indeed a real-time challenge not only for India but for many developing and even developed countries. All nations with the exception of most advanced ones like some European countries, USA, Russia, China, and Australia are under the new threat of colonization by companies. Many nations have already become the slaves of companies like the Google, Microsoft, Yahoo, Amazon, Flipkart, Twitters, Facebook, WhatsApp, and so on which offer free services, and people are addictively accustomed to using them, round the clock, and contributing to app-based economy of these enterprises. So much so not a day passes without using these; in the process we only enrich such companies to swiftly become millionaires and even billionaires. Such developments are consequent to digital revolution, high-speed Wi-Fi services and creation of networks of people, things, services, and machine learning, AI and so on. These developments have given rise to many challenges and, for less developed nations they have almost become the battle grounds. Obviously, newer ways of colonization (e.g. digital colonization) by companies rather than by nations have already emerged. However, colonization of nations by companies is not entirely a new phenomenon. Recall the familiar 'East India Company'. It was a mere joint-stock business company which following the 1st Industrial Revolution (IR 1.0) called the 'Textile Revolution' dominated the world for nearly 200 years. It was indeed more powerful than any country of its time (see Malhotra, 2021 for detailed discussion on the impacts of AI).

Briefly stated, the implications of AI and machine learning are far greater than most people would like to believe or perceive. Digital revolution and ownership of digital facilities by companies today affect our privacy, data security, day-to-day activities in all spheres of our life, besides the nation's international relations, and border security. Sadly, and ironically machines are getting smarter and people are getting dumber. Memory power and ability to compute are vanishing steadily. Therefore, outsourcing critical thinking and data storage using digital devices has become inevitable. Unfathomable learning capacities of machines are making human beings progressively shallow in knowledge. Furthermore, there seems to be in general, a loss in cognitive skills and ability to concentrate for longer times following our increased dependence on machines. It appears as if Lamarckism is working as far as his 'use and disuse' theory is concerned. Long before Charles Darwin, who gave the world a profound 'Theory of Evolution' (in 1858); Jean Baptist Lamarck (in 1801) had postulated that disuse of organs leads to degeneration. Indeed, this can happen. For example, muscle wasting results following lack of activity. Luckily, somatic changes are not heritable to the offspring and the principles of inheritance were unknown during the time of Lamarck. Returning to the impact of AI and machine learning, is it possible that increasing use of these tools in a way diminishing our brainpowers? It appears to be so. Evidently, dependency on machines has led to the loss of computational skills, and memory in human beings. For instance, before the advent of calculators, complex mathematics was done using human brains. Before the mobile phones arrived we could remember a good number of telephone numbers of our near and dear ones, friends and relatives. But now most people struggle to remember their own telephone numbers. Obviously, to keep up the cognitive skills and enhance memory power of our brain (human hard disk), we should revive some of our ancient practices like memorizing multiplication tables, remembering aphorisms, verses, mantras and so on composed by eminent ancient scholars, written in regional languages, Sanskrit, Urdu and English at least during the school education.

The AI has wide ranging applications and impact on human activities. So much so, the digital gadgets and AI are replacing human tasks and creating job disruptions with unimaginable consequences. Many types of jobs (blue- or white-collared) are regularly disappearing or becoming out-dated. Also, the digital divide between different groups of people is quite wide. During the recent Covid-19 pandemic, when the nation attempted to conduct classes online, the digital divides and inadequacy of high-speed internet and access to digital devices and expertise of teachers and learners became very obvious. Digital divides are commonly seen between the rich and the poor, rural and urban, urban-rich and urban-poor and so on. However, the digital divides are not restricted to only between the haves and have-nots. It is seen even between the teachers and the learners where the latter may be more advanced than the former. All such divides can lead to social instabilities and disequilibrium. Notwithstanding all this, future is hugely poised to embrace AI in a big way. Therefore, great caution and alertness are needed. The Russian President Vladimir Putin once opined that "Artificial Intelligence is the future, and not only for Russia, but for all humankind. It comes with colossal opportunities, but also threats that are difficult to predict. Whoever becomes the leader in this sphere will become the ruler of the world". The recent book *Artificial Intelligence and the Future of Power* (Malhotra, 2021) analyses the consequences of AI in detail. An issue of great concern is that AI can come handy to those interested in breaking India to create hatred and hostile groups of people to fight among themselves, and the country. The piercing message of such developments is that revamping higher education is the pressing need to endure looming global challenges, overcome misuse of AI, cybercrimes, and reduce the impact of colonization by companies.

To sum up, soul-searching from any angle, unequivocally suggests that restructuring the Indian education system (schools to universities) and taking it to international standards is inevitable.

For this to happen, remodeling universities, and repurposing higher education is the only solution. However, numerous challenges will surface that will have to be conquered. Therefore, the nation must recognize the importance of *competency* in teaching, learning and assessment processes, and overall management of higher education from colleges to regulatory bodies. All this will require a change in the mind set of academicians as well as politicians, and policies of the regulatory bodies. First, the appointment of various heads, the leaders (the principals, vice chancellors, chairpersons of various regulatory bodies, etc.) and the faculty, competency and record of accomplishment should prevail over seniority and minimum basic qualifications. Second, the State/Central Governments may facilitate the HEIs to establish a 'state of the art' infrastructure. High speed, uninterrupted Wi-Fi facilities should become common and affordable to both rural and urban dwellers regardless of their financial status. Third, the existing teachers need retraining or relearning for adoption of modern pedagogies of teaching, learning, and assessment, practiced internationally. Fourth, the future curriculums of various courses have to be *context* based with clear strategies of *content* delivery. Fifth, the government must make up its mind to restore total autonomy to universities, and invest liberally to harvest dividends later. Sixth, scanty investment in education will ensure little dividends and jeopardize the national interests. There are ways to find resources. Alumni and donors may be encouraged with liberal income tax incentives to donate funds for rebuilding the universities. Spending on various conferences could be on hold, say for five years. Likewise, funding for research may be limited to only nationally relevant and need based projects and development of technologies. Lastly, all industries may be cajoled to have tie-up with universities for not only research but also for manufacturing products as described earlier in this book.

In the university system as in the private enterprises and industries, right people need to be in right place (academics or administration). Only then the desired outcome may be expected. The HEIs also need to be managed on the principles of private sectors through competent CEOs (call them Principals/Vice Chancellors) with hire and fire provisions to weed out those who fail to deliver goods. Mere application of democratic principles and recruitment of personnel (teaching or supporting) on considerations other than competency and usefulness to the institutions will further ruin education scenario. Lee Kuan Yew the former Prime Minister and Father of modern Singapore once stated that "What a country needs to develop is discipline more than democracy. The exuberance of democracy leads to undisciplined and disorderly conditions which are inimical to development". Equity, access and excellence are good slogans. But all these can rarely go together. Will Durant, the author of *The Lessons of History* aptly stated that "In progressive societies the concentration [of wealth] may reach a point where the strength of number in the many poor rivals the strength of ability in the few rich; then the unstable equilibrium generates a critical situation, which history has diversely met by legislation redistributing wealth or by revolution, distributing poverty". Moreover, in India, Gresham's Law has operated for too long, driving merited and competent people out of India from which other nations have gained. A good example is the fact that the home-grown Indians, as many as six are CEOs of top technology industries of the world as of now: Microsoft, Google, IBM, Adobe, Palo Alto Networks, and Twitter. Is this not enough testimony of scholarship, commitment, and capability of those born and brought-up in India?

Closing Comments: It is gratifying that at present the country is obsessed with the NEP 2020, which provides hope and optimism for resurrection and modernization of education system in India. A moot question is, are we ready to take hard measures? I do not know. But, hard measures will alone help in remodeling the universities and resurrecting the vibrancy of academic ecosystems. Political considerations should not come in the way of implementing the new education policy. At the same time, implementing NEP 2020 shoddily or in a hurry will do little good. A missed opportunity can result in the irreparable damage to the nation. This book is a step in the direction of remodeling higher education and management of universities which need to align themselves with the current national and global trends and challenges. The universities now more than ever need to produce graduates who are not merely future ready with required skills, but with ability to think creatively and capable of innovating. As the welfare of our nation and the society solely depend upon the quality of education, it is not enough to be seized of NEP 2020 and challenges in its implementation, we need to seize it. A nation fails when its universities fail.

Lastly, churning out myriads of certificates and degrees by universities without due regard to relevance, quality, and credentials will be a futile exercise. Heart of the matter is quality education that clearly spearheads development of *life skills* and or *livelihood skills* rather than preparing the learners merely for higher (degree) classes. The 'life skills' include: creative and critical thinking, solving problems, ability for communication, management, taking decision, understanding personal and social responsibilities and so on. The 'livelihood skills' include developing technical and professional or vocational skills (e.g. engineering, carpentry, plumbing, electrical/civil works, catering, nutrition management, and numerous such other talents). A new challenge of the future is that in future, one cannot predict the nature of future jobs. For all probability, there will not be permanent jobs in the future. If so, all jobs will be temporary in nature. Hence, universities have to take a cognizance of such potentially possible projections while designing the curricula for various degree courses. Though NEP 2020 provides hope for reforming the education system, it is not enough to have a good screenplay; we need good directors and actors to play the drama, not merely to entertain the audience but also to enlighten them and give meaning to the story and philosophy embedded in it. As a word of caution, in the absence of political will, liberal funding, and greater participation of the academic community in the remodeling of universities, it will be incredibly difficult to reform Indian education system.

Works Cited

Case, S. (2016). *The Third Wave—An Entrepreneurs Vision of the Future*. Simon & Schuster, NY.

Chaddah, P. (2018). "Ethics in Competitive Research". Pothi.com

Chandra, P. (2017). *Building Universities that Matter*. Orient Black Swan Pvt. Ltd., Hyderabad.

Ghosh, M. (2019a). "Stress Management". In *Management of Collegiate Education in the 21st Century: Some Insights* (Ed. S.K. Saidapur), pp. 269-80, Gyan Books, New Delhi.

—— (2019b). "Counselling Students". In *Management of Collegiate Education in the 21st Century: Some Insights* (Ed. S.K. Saidapur), pp. 281-96, Gyan Books, New Delhi.

Joshi, A. (2019). "Library: A Learning Resource Centre". In *Management of Collegiate Education in the 21st Century: Some Insights* (Ed. S.K. Saidapur), pp. 235-44, Gyan Books, New Delhi.

Muralidhar, K., Ghosh, A, Singhvi, A.K. (2019). *Ethics in Science Education, Research and Governance*. Indian National Science Academy, New Delhi.

Malhotra, R. (2021). *Artificial Intelligence and the Future of Power*. Rupa Publications, New Delhi.

Pathania, G.J. (2018). *The University as a Site of Resistance—Identity and Student Politics*. Oxford University Press, New Delhi.

Saidapur, S.K. (2017). "Revamping Higher Education". Guest Editorial. *Current Science*, vol. 113, 831-32.

—— (2019a). "Value of Higher Education and Role of Teachers". In *Management of Collegiate Education in the 21st*

Century: Some Insights (Ed. S.K. Saidapur), pp. 31-40, Gyan Books, New Delhi.

—— (2019b). "Leadership Role of Principals". In *Management of Collegiate Education in the 21st Century: Some Insights* (Ed. S.K. Saidapur), pp. 133-52, Gyan Books, New Delhi.

—— (2019c). "Education in the 21st Century". In *Management of Collegiate Education in the 21st Century: Some Insights* (Ed. S.K. Saidapur), pp. 325-32, Gyan Books, New Delhi.

—— (2019d). "Redesigning Higher Education: A few Titbits". In *Management of Collegiate Education in the 21st Century: Some Insights* (Ed. S.K. Saidapur), pp. 333-48, Gyan Books, New Delhi.

—— (2020a). "Trends in the 21st Century Education". *Univ. News*, vol. 58, pp. 3-10.

—— (2020b). "Role of teachers in changing educational scenario". Karnatak University, Journal, *Science*, vol. 51, pp. 1-10.

—— (2021). "NEP: Curriculum Development Holds Key". *Deccan Herald*, July 19, 2021.

Sathyanarayana, N.V. (2019). "From clay tablet to digital tablet: Towards ideal library". In *Management of Collegiate Education in the 21st Century: Some Insights* (Ed. S.K. Saidapur), pp. 223-34, Gyan Books, New Delhi.

Shanbhag, A.B. (2019a). "Progression of higher education in the post-independent India". In *Management of Collegiate Education in the 21st Century: Some Insights* (Ed. S.K. Saidapur), pp. 53-92, Gyan Books, New Delhi.

—— (2019b). "Involving alumni in college development". In *Management of Collegiate Education in the 21st Century: Some Insights* (Ed. S.K. Saidapur), pp. 313-24, Gyan Books, New Delhi.

Thyagarajan, S.P. (2019). "Brief history of Indian higher education". In *Management of Collegiate Education in the 21st Century: Some Insights* (Ed. S.K. Saidapur), pp. 41-52, Gyan Books, New Delhi.

Varghese, M. Katre S., and Reddy, S. (2019). *Dynamics of Indian Higher Education*. Abhijeet Publications, New Delhi.

Further Reading

1. *Sri Aurobindo and the Mother on Education* (1956). Sri Aurobindo Ashram Trust, Puducherry.
2. Gautier, F. (2013). *A History of India As It Happened—Not As It Has Been Written*. Har-Anand Publishers, Pvt. Ltd., New Delhi.
3. Sharma, K.A. (2013). *Sixty Years of the University Grants Commission: Establishment, Growth and Evolution*. UGC, New Delhi.
4. "National Education Policy 2020". Report of Ministry of Human Resource Development, Government of India, New Delhi.
5. GUNI Report 6. (2017): Higher Education in the World. Towards a Socially Responsible University: Balancing the Global with the Local.
6. Good Academic Research Practices—Guidance Report, (2020). University Grants Commission, New Delhi.
7. *Revamping Science Education in Karnataka*. Department of Science & Technology, Government of Karnataka, 2021. www.kstacademy.in

Notes

1. ***Modern pedagogies***: Examples include: Combination of Online and Offline Teaching-Learning Processes (Blended learning), Use of Flipped classrooms, Virtual lecture halls and labs, Webinars, Seminars, Use of Online Platforms, Various Apps, Group learning, Project-based learning, Self-learning, Quizzes, Content creation and sharing, Solving solved and Unsolved Problems, Creative and Critical thinking etc.
2. ***Courses***: There exists considerable variation in the perception of terms like the *'Discipline, Open Electives, Add on courses, Intra—and Interdisciplinary, Multidisciplinary and Trans-disciplinary'* and so on among the academia. However, these terms are used extensively and sometimes indiscriminately. An attempt is made here to provide an opinion on the above terms as shown below:
   - (i) ***Discipline***: A major subject domain with clear boundaries (e.g. Physics, Zoology, Botany, History, Mathematics, Sociology, etc.). Therefore, narrow specialized areas like say 'Toxicology', 'Plant Tissue Culture', 'Biostatistics', 'Mathematical Modeling', 'Systems Biology', 'Genetics', 'Biochemistry', 'Nano-chemistry', 'Corporate Social Responsibility' and so on do not constitute disciplines, in the real sense. They can be regarded as sub-disciplines.
   - (ii) ***Intra-disciplinary/inter-disciplinary***: Many subject domains are fragmented today giving rise to numerous sub-disciplines or areas of study. A good example is 'Biology'. It was first fragmented

into Botany, Zoology, and Microbiology. Later fragmented into numerous branches like: Entomology, Anatomy, Physiology, Parasitology, Protozoology, Freshwater Zoology, Marine Biology, Developmental Biology, Genetics, Aquaculture, Fish Biology, Fisheries, Biochemistry, Biophysics, Biotechnology, Chronobiology, Cancer Biology, Cell Biology, Radiation Biology, Endocrinology, Immunology, Molecular Biology, Toxicology, Environmental Biology, Wildlife Biology, Evolutionary Biology, and so on to name a few. The major benefit was creating new 'Departments' by equating such fragmented pieces of biology as 'Disciplines'. This promoted research and procurement of research grants in certain specialized areas but at the cost of understanding the intricacies, complexities and 'conceptualization' of the complex biological systems in their entirety. Now there is a cry to bring fragmented areas (the sub-disciplines) back in the fold of biology through integration of subjects in the guise of 'interdisciplinary' approach. Similar is the case with other science, arts and social science subjects including the languages. One wonders if there are any fields with clear-cut boundaries that qualify to be called as *interdisciplinary* subject(s) and whether they can be accorded the status of a 'Discipline' in the real sense. Overlapping of areas between different subject areas is almost always possible. At the same time, fixity of boundaries between subjects is progressively eroding. In view of rapid developments and growth of almost all subject domains, a kind of integration of closely or distantly related subjects hitherto kept out of certain disciplines is needed. As an example, study of biomolecules is an inseparable part of biology and it calls for integration of biochemistry with biology. Similarly, biophysical aspects have to be to be integrated with biology. To give another good example: the study of 'Immuno-pharmacology' makes sense when it is integrated with fields like the 'bacteriology, physiology, genetics, immunology, and chemistry'.

On the side of the Social Sciences, subjects like 'Anthropology', 'Sociology', and 'Social Work' need to be integrated and the newly evolved course could be renamed possible as 'Evolution of Human Societies'. Likewise, a judicious combination of subjects like the 'History', 'Archaeology', 'Epigraphy' and related domains can go together as 'Historical Sciences'. And 'Economics', 'Commerce', 'Banking and Management' could be integrated under a discipline as 'Trade and Business Management'. Modernizing the curriculum of higher education system through such integrations can lead to better conceptualizations. Further, it may lead to much needed *transcended* knowledge.

(iii) ***Multidisciplinary***: This approach is best suited for research rather than for teaching. A multidisciplinary approach involves team works and collaborations with people of different subject domains/expertise, to tackle intricate problems.

(iv) ***Trans-disciplinary Research***: It technically means a practice that transgresses and transcends disciplinary boundaries (e.g. Marxism, Structuralism and Feminist Theory). It is not as simple as defining *cis* and *trans* isomers in the field of chemistry. In the context of higher education 'trans' should denote something 'beyond' and not just 'across'. Researches involving a judicious mix of different disciplines of science and/or social sciences domain leading to new transcended knowledge, new postulations, concepts, models, hypotheses or theories, and methodological uses constitute *trans-disciplinary* research. For example, religion and philosophy along with say yoga and meditation may lead to transcended knowledge. Similarly, integrated approach to the study of history, archaeology and epigraphy may shed new transcended knowledge hitherto not known to man. Such approaches represent trans-disciplinary research. In short, trans-disciplinary research is a higher order pursuit. It is not a mere interdisciplinary research. Therefore, making a clear distinction between interdisciplinary and trans-disciplinary nature of research is very much warranted.

3. ***Open Electives***: These are specially designed courses by one department, by and large for the benefit of students of other departments, available across the faculties. These may include basic science courses for students of Arts, Humanities and Social Sciences. Similarly courses from Liberal Arts may be made available to Science students. The various Departments may offer the choice of special papers for their own students; but these need not be called open electives.
4. ***Add-on Courses***: Such courses should ideally help students to get additional training in skill development (e.g. communication, etc.), Science Journalism, and Functional use of a language, study of a Foreign Language, Making Documentaries and Editing Videos, Web Designing, Corporate Social Responsibility (CSR), Accounting, Computing Income Tax Returns, and Personality Development and so on. Likewise, courses on 'Indian Society', 'Brief History of India', 'Great Indian Epics and Heritage', 'International Affairs', 'Management of Water Bodies', 'Horticulture', 'Floriculture', 'Civic Sense and Public Hygiene', 'Tourism', 'Tele Marketing', 'Disaster Management', etc., can be very useful.
5. ***Purpose of Integration of Subjects***: Integration of closely related courses that enhance understanding a basic discipline or subject area is of paramount importance. Such an exercise should lead to evolving entirely new courses and developing holistic approach to a given subject domain (see examples cited above). As far as the languages are concerned, at PG level, it is possible to study one semester of local/regional language, one semester of

Sanskrit, one semester of Hindi and one semester of any foreign language. Such integrations through redesigned courses can go a long way on enhancing the perception and command over the language, as well as employability of the learners.

6. ***Liberal Arts/Liberal Education***: It is rather a difficult issue and not easy to design liberal education programs. Mere provision of unrelated courses will not amount to liberal education. Ideally or philosophically, liberal education is supposed to help expand ones horizons and ability to communicate with ease—say fluency of language, ability for critical and analytical reasoning, and coping up with new or unforeseen (challenging) situations and so on. In short, liberal education is considered essential to the well-educated persons to enable them to participate in civic life.

   Caveat: The above ideas are only indicative and provocative. More deliberations are needed to arrive at a consensus at the national level.

Appendices

Appendix–1

Delegation of Administrative and Financial Powers

(Appendix to Chapter–2)

The following passages illustrate the nature of administrative and financial powers that can be delegated to various officers of the university. Such provisions are operational in Karnatak University since the year 2007. These were framed under the Karnataka State Universities (KSU) Act, 2000, Statute 29(2) (a) and (n) Statute 17(1), and (4) vide Syndicate resolutions (i) No. 12 dated 14.12.2006 and (ii) No. 66 dated 14.7.2007. Varsities desirous of decentralizing administration can up these ideas and further refine them. Advantage of delegating powers is that actions taken by respective officers (as per the provision) do not require further ratification from the governing bodies of the universities. It brings in transparency, ensures fast clearance of files and reduces mundane works of higher authorities.

Delegation of Administrative Powers to:

Vice–Chancellor

1. To sanction promotions to Class IV to III in the promotional quota as per C&R Rules and State University Act.
2. To confirm University Employees after satisfactory completion of probation as per State University Act—Syndicate is the competitive authority.
3. To sanction time scale increment to teaching staff.

4. To appoint tabulators, coding officers, custodian, dispatch officers, Chief Superintendent and the Deputy Chief Superintendents and examination hall reviewers (invigilators, clerical assistants, typist, etc.) as per rules.
5. To sanction remuneration to various officers/officials involved in coding, tabulating, invigilation, typing, supervision, clerical job, and laboratory assistants etc., as per rules.
6. To permit extra cost by way of travelling allowance and hotel allowance under special circumstances.
7. To sanction retirement benefit to the university employees.
8. To sanction daily allowance for halts not exceeding 30 days and determine the shortest route within the state.
9. To fix the amount of security required from a university employee as per rules.
10. To accord administrative sanction for civil works.
    (A) Original works for roads, buildings, water supply and drainages (up to Rs. One Lakh).
    (B) Ordinary repairs.
11. To accord administrative approval for lump sum provision in the sanctioned estimates for civil works.
12. To accord administrative approval for Annual Maintenance Estimates (up to Rupees One Lakh) in respect of (A) Water supply & sanitary, (B) Electricity, and (C) Roads.
13. To accord administrative approval and technical sanctions to the revised or modified estimates up to 25% over the original sanctioned cost.
14. To sanction expenditure on urgent repairs to buildings, roads, water supply, and electricity installations etc. subject to budget provisions.
15. Acceptance of tenders after observing all formalities.
16. To execute and conclude all agreements and contract documents in connection with all works for which approval has been given by the higher authorities pertaining to the University Engineering Division.

17. To authorize signing and acceptance of 'Tenders and Quotations'.
18. To sanction advertisement charges for Tender Notifications in newspapers by charging it to the works concerned.

Registrar

1. To sanction all types of leave up to three months duration, to subordinate employees, including leave refusal, and leave surrender (except special disability leave, extra-ordinary and study leave).
2. To sanction maternity and paternity leave as per rules.
3. To sanction time scale increment to all classes of non-teaching staff.
4. To execute and conclude all agreements and contracts with the approval of the appropriate authorities.
5. To sign, on behalf of the university, bills, notes, receipts, acceptances, endorsements, cheques, release agreements, contracts and documents and to authorize signing and acceptance.
6. To order retirement of all employees who have attained the age of superannuation.
7. To sanction retirement benefit to the Group C & D employees.
8. To sanction daily allowance for halts not exceeding 30 days and to declare the shortest route within the state for Group C & D employees.
9. To sanction DCRG/Gratuity to families of university employees as per rules.
10. To accord administrative sanction for civil works.
    (A) Original works for roads, buildings, water supply and drainage (up to ₹ 50,000).
    (B) Ordinary repairs (₹ 50,000 at a time and maximum ₹ 5,00,000 per annum).
11. To sanction expenditure on urgent repairs to university buildings, roads, water supply, and electricity installations

etc. subject to the budget provisions up to ₹ 50,000 at a time and maximum ₹ 5,00,000 per annum.

12. According administrative approval for Annual Maintenance Estimates in respect of
    (A) Water supply and sanitary, (B) Electricity, and (C) Roads. ₹ 50,000 in each case.
13. Issue of Tender notifications/Quotations with detailed specifications for all works following approval by the appropriate authorities.
14. Acceptance of Tenders after observing all formalities.
15. To execute and conclude all agreements and contract documents of all works (pertaining to the University Engineering Division) for which approval is given by the appropriate authorities.
16. To sanction charges for taking photographs of the works and advertisement charges for Tender notifications by charging it to the works concerned.
17. To sanction purchase of blue-printing paper, ammonia ink, etc. by charging it to the sanctioned works.
18. To issue notification in respect of newly affiliated colleges after approval of the Syndicate/Executive Council.

Registrar (Evaluation)

1. To appoint tabulators, coding officers, custodian, dispatch officers Chief Superintendent and the deputy chief superintendents and examination hall reviewers (invigilators, clerical assistants, typist, etc.) as per rules.
2. To sanction remuneration to the various officers/officials involved in coding, tabulating, invigilation, typing, supervision, clerical job, and laboratory assistants etc., as per rules.
3. To permit a person to write answer scripts for Blind candidates, as per rules.
4. To sanction extra time to write answers for physically challenged candidates, as per rules.

Finance Officer

1. To allow time scale increment to all classes of teaching and non-teaching staff on due date, excepting the cases for which university has given directions to withhold increments. The Finance Officer shall intimate to the DPAR Section/concerned Head of the Sections for having released the annual increment for entry in the Service Register of concerned employees.
2. To sanction temporary advances from the university contributory provident fund or GPF as per rules, up to ₹ 50,000.
3. To sanction partial and permanent withdrawals from the University General Provident Fund as per rules.

Delegation of Financial Powers to:

Vice-Chancellor

1. To sanction retirement benefits to Group A & B employees of the university in case of death or attainment of the age of superannuation (including DCRG's).
2. To sanction reimbursement of medical charges as per rules.
3. To sanction cost of advertisement in approved news media.
4. To sanction expenditures in respect of purchase of spares, tyre and tubes etc. minor overhauls & major and minor repairs to university vehicles in accordance with the laid down rules.
5. To sanction expenditure on tea and refreshments for official meetings, visitors, etc.
6. To sanction procurement of new telephones.
7. To sanction laboratory equipment and chemicals to university departments up to ₹ 1,00,000.
8. To accord sanction for purchases of equipment other than laboratory equipment up to ₹ 1,00,000 at a time.
9. To sanction furniture, fittings, etc. to university departments, officers, university colleges, teaching

departments, hostels and other subordinate departments up to ₹ 1,00,000 at a time.

10. To sanction for printing of departmental forms, graduation lists, convocation forms, degree certificates, registers, eligibility lists, candidates lists and other printing works.
11. To sanction local purchase of stationery articles in case of exigencies up to a maximum of ₹ 40,000 at a time.
12. To sanction repair of clocks, time pieces, computers, typewriters, etc. as per rules.
13. To sanction TA advances to all categories of university employees.
14. To sanction proceed on duty within the State or outside the State but within India.
15. To sanction non-recurring contingent expenditures.
16. To sanction refund of tuition fee and other fees paid by the students and refund of registration fees, affiliation fees, etc.
17. To sanction refund of EMD and other security deposits, as per rules.
18. To sanction shifting charges as per rules (Departments, Allied Offices, etc.).
19. To sanction payment of time barred claims preferred by other departments regarding supply and services.
20. To sanction the destruction of time barred records as per rules—full powers as per State Finance Code.
21. To sanction the hiring of building, furniture, etc. to conduct examinations.
22. To sanction purchase of diaries and other table equipment to officers of the university not below the rank of Assistant Registrar or equivalent cadre.
23. To sanction expenditure on binding of books, journals, periodicals, registers, etc.
24. To sanction conveyance charges within cities (to persons on office work) and for field studies for investigators of research projects as per rules.

25. To sanction legal charges like court fee and other charges.
26. To sanction awards other than research awards to the university employees where due diligence and discretion were used in order to protect/promote/university property/interest.
27. To sanction expenditure towards purchase of dictionaries, reference books, etc. for office use.
28. To countersign bills.
29. To sanction remuneration/honorarium/royalty to authors/reviewers/Professors/Readers, etc.
30. To sanction expenditure in connection with the manufacture of blocks, art work, etc.
31. To subscribe newspapers, journals, periodicals up to ₹ 1,0000 P.A.
32. To sanction payment of honorarium to the speakers, guest lecturers, etc.
33. To sanction repair charges of machinery in Computer Units/USIC/Workshop, etc.
34. To sanction expenditure in connection with the exhibition of books, special lectures, extension lectures, endowment lectures, etc.
35. To sanction Air Fare to Board of Examiners, Board of Appointment/Board of Studies/Extramural Studies/Student welfare and other invitees and employees.
36. To sanction drugs, minor equipment, etc. to the Health Centres.
37. To sanction contingent amount in connection with the university examinations as per rules.

Registrar

1. To sanction retirement benefits to Group C & D employees of the university in case of death or attaining the age of superannuation (including DCRG's).
2. To sanction reimbursement of medical charges up to ₹ 25,000 as per rules.

3. To sanction cost of advertisement in approved news media.
4. To sanction expenditures in respect of purchase of spares, tubes and tubes, etc., minor overhauls and major and minor repairs to university vehicles in accordance with the rules laid down.
5. To sanction expenditure for tea and refreshments on official meetings, visitors, etc. up to ₹ 50,000.
6. To sanction shifting charges of telephones.
7. To sanction laboratory equipment and chemicals to university departments up to ₹ 50,000.
8. To sanction purchase of equipment other than laboratory equipment ₹ 50,000 at a time.
9. To sanction furniture, fittings, etc. to university departments, offices, university colleges, teaching departments, hostels and other subordinate departments up to ₹ 50,000.
10. To sanction printing of departmental forms graduation lists, convocation forms, degree certificates, registers, eligibility lists, candidates lists and other printing works ₹ 20,000 at a time.
11. To sanction local purchase of stationery articles in case of exigencies ₹ 10,000 each case.
12. To sanction repair of clocks, timepieces, typewrites, etc. ₹ 10,000 at a time.
13. To sanction TA advances to all the categories of employees of the university except that of the Chairpersons of the departments (COD).
14. To sanction proceed on duty within the State or outside the State but within India (for other than CODs/ Principals).
15. To sanction non-recurring contingent expenditure ₹ 10,000 at a time.
16. To sanction refund of tuition and other fees paid by the students and refund of registration fees, affiliation fees, etc. up to ₹ 10,000.

17. To sanction refund of EMD amount and other deposits, as per rules.
18. To sanction festival advances to the university employees as per rules.
19. To sanction shifting charges as per rules (Departments, Offices, etc.) up to ₹ 20,000 per annum.
20. To sanction payment of time barred claims by other departments regarding supply and services up to ₹ 20,000 within three years in each case.
21. To sanction destruction of time barred records as per rules—full powers as per State Finance Code.
22. To sanction purchase of diaries and other table equipment to officers of the university not below the rank of Assistant Registrar or equivalent cadre up to ₹ 20,000 per annum.
23. To sanction expenditure on binding of books, journals, periodicals, registers, etc. ₹ 10,000 in each case.
24. To sanction conveyance charges within cities (for persons on office work) as per rules ₹ 2,000 in each case and ₹ 20,000 per annum.
25. To sanction legal charges like court fee and other charges—as per approved rates.
26. To sanction awards other than research awards to the university employees where due diligence and discretion were used in order to protect/promote/university property/ interest ₹ 1,000 each case and ₹ 8,000 per annum.
27. To sanction expenditures towards purchase of dictionaries, reference books, etc. for office use.
28. To countersign bills.
29. To sanction remuneration/honorarium/royalty to authors/ reviewers/Professors Readers, etc.
30. To sanction expenditure in connection with manufacture of blocks, art work, etc. up to ₹ 10,000 at a time.
31. To subscribe newspapers, journals, periodicals up to ₹ 5,000.

Registrar (Evaluation)

1. To sanction expenditures in respect of purchase of spares, tyre and tubes, etc. minor overhauls and major and minor repairs to vehicles under his charge, in accordance with the rules laid down up to ₹ 5,000 at a time and ₹ 20,000 per annum.
2. To sanction expenditure for tea and refreshments on official meetings, visitors, etc. ₹ 1,000 at a time.
3. To accord sanction for purchase of equipment concerning his branch up to ₹ 10,000 at a time (maximum ₹ 40,000 per annum).
4. To sanction for printing of departmental forms graduation lists, convocation forms, degree certificates, registers, eligibility lists, candidates lists and other printing works ₹ 20,000 at a time.
5. To sanction local purchase of stationery articles in case of exigencies ₹ 10,000 each case.
6. To sanction repair of clocks, time pieces, typewriters, etc. of the examination section as per rules ₹ 500 at a time.
7. To sanction TA advances to all categories of employees pertaining to examination section.
8. To sanction to proceed on duty, group C and D employees of his section (within and outside the state).
9. To sanction non-recurring contingent expenditure ₹ 5,000 at a time.
10. To sanction destruction of time barred records as per rules—full powers as per rules.
11. To sanction the hiring of building, furniture, etc. to conduct Examinations ₹ 20,000 at a time in case of furniture—maximum ₹ 20,000 per annum.
12. To sanction expenditure on binding of books, documents, registers, etc. ₹ 10,000 pertaining to his section.
13. To sanction conveyance charges within cities (for persons on office work) as per rules ₹ 2,000 in each case and ₹ 20,000 per annum.

14. To sanction expenditure towards purchase of dictionaries, reference books, etc. for office use ₹ 1,000 at a time—maximum ₹ 6,000 per annum.
15. To countersign bills.
16. To subscribe newspapers up to ₹ 5,000 per annum.
17. To sanction contingent amount in connection with the university examinations as per rules ₹ 10,000 at a time.
18. Sanction of TA/DA to members of the various examination related boards as per rules.
19. To grant advances for valuation/Chief Coordinators, etc. for various post graduate examinations up to ₹ 1 Lakh at a time.

Finance Officer

1. To sanction expenditures in respect of purchase of spares, tyres and tubes, etc. minor overhauls and major and minor repairs to university vehicles in accordance with the rules laid down up to ₹ 5,000 at a time and ₹ 20,000 per annum to the controlling Officers in-charge of the vehicle.
2. To sanction expenditure for tea and refreshments on official meetings, visitors, etc. ₹ 1,000 at a time.
3. To accord sanction for purchase of equipment concerning his branch ₹ 10,000 at a time.
4. To sanction local purchase of stationery articles in case of exigencies ₹ 1,000 each case and not exceeding ₹ 5,000 per annum.
5. To sanction repair of clocks, time pieces, computers, typewriters, etc. pertaining to Finance Section as per rules ₹ 500 at a time.
6. To sanction proceed on duty within the State and outside the State within India group C and D employees of his department.
7. To sanction non-recurring contingent expenditure ₹ 5,000 at a time.

8. To sanction destruction of time barred records as per rules—full powers as per rules.
9. To sanction expenditure on binding of books, registers, etc. ₹ 2,000 in each case of her/his section.
10. To sanction conveyance charges within cities (for persons on office work) as per rules ₹ 2,000 in each case, maximum ₹ 20,000 per annum, to employees of his section.
11. To sanction expenditure towards purchase of dictionaries, reference books, etc. of office use ₹ 1,000 at a time, maximum of ₹ 6,000 per annum.
12. To countersign bills.
13. To grant GPF advances/partial withdrawal up to ₹ 50,000 by following applicable rules.

Librarian

1. To sanction local purchases of stationery articles ₹ 5,000 at a time.
2. To sanction repairs to clocks, furniture and any other articles of the library ₹ 1,000 at a time.
3. To sanction expenditure in connection with the binding of books and journals, records, etc. including purchase of materials required for binding ₹ 5,000 at a time.
4. To sanction local purchase of pencils, broom-sticks, washing powders, insecticides, etc. for the maintenance of office and library/cloak room ₹ 1,000 at a time, not exceeding ₹ 4,000 per annum.
5. Passing bills pertaining to library and countersigning whenever necessary.
6. To draw salary and allowances of the office establishment under his control.
7. To sanction time-scale increments of employees working under his control automatic.
8. To sanction casual leave to employees working in library.

9. To sanction of earned leave, half-pay leave and other kind of leave to employees working under him up to two months in a Calendar year.
10. To sanction of maternity and paternity leave to staff working in library as per rules.
11. To auction unserviceable articles as per the conditions stipulated by the university not exceeding the original cost of ₹ 2,000 of articles.
12. To incur expenditure relating to the purchase of books, journals, periodicals, etc. as per norms of the university: (A) Renewal of subscriptions; (B) purchase of books and non-book materials on the recommendations of concerned Head of the Department/Chairman of the Department subject to the allocation of funds by the Library Advisory Board; (C) To take subscription to journals on the recommendation of HOD/COD and Library Advisory Board—Subject to allocation of funds by the Library Advisory Board up to ₹ 50,000 per annum.
13. To utilize imprest advance for the purpose of incurring expenditure for the maintenance of office up to ₹ 5,000 annually.
14. To make specific recommendations to the university regarding the award of punishment to students for the indiscipline, misbehaviour and misuse of library facilities.
15. To sanction festival advances to library staff as per rules.

Chairpersons of PG Departments/Administrators of PG Centres

1. To sanction local purchase of stationery and other articles like soap, detergents/insecticides, washing powder, etc. up to ₹ 1,000 at a time.
2. To sanction repairs to clocks, furniture and any of other articles of office/laboratory equipment ₹ 1,000 at a time. For repair of scientific equipment ₹ 10,000 at a time.
3. To sanction purchase of laboratory subject to the provisions contained under budget with the usual procedure ₹ 10,000 at a time.

4. To sanction expenditure in connection with the binding of books and journals, records, etc. ₹ 1,000 per annum.
5. To countersign bills other than establishment, T.A. and other bills.
6. To purchase reference books, manuals, etc. for office use ₹ 1,000 at a time.
7. To sanction educational tour, annual leadership training, camp-nicks and picnics and specimen collection tours as per rules.
8. To sanction casual leave to employees of the department/ PG centre.

Director, Publication Division (Prasaranga)

1. To sanction casual leave in respect of the staff of Prasaranga.
2. To permit officers and other officials working under him, to proceed on duty within the State.
3. To sanction local purchases of stationery articles ₹ 500 at a time.
4. To sanction repairs of furniture and other articles including computers, typewriters and duplicators as per rules ₹ 500 at a time.
5. To sanction non-recurring contingent expenditure up to ₹ 500 at a time.
6. To sanction purchase of books and periodicals required in connection with publication as per rules—not exceeding ₹ 1,000 in respect of one publication.
7. To sanction expenditure in connection with manufacture of blocs art work at the approved rates up to ₹ 5,000 at a time.
8. To sanction expenses connected with the printing works to private printers at the approved rates after observing rules up to ₹ 5,000.
9. To sanction remuneration/honorarium to speakers/royalty to authors/reviewers/proofreaders at the approved rates

approved by the university authorities up to ₹ 5,000 at a time.

10. To sanction and incur expenditure on items pertaining to extension lectures, special lectures and endowment lectures such as TA and DA to the respective officials, seating arrangements, microphones, tape recording, photographs and garlands as per norms.
11. To incur expenditure on advertisements as per rules up to ₹ 2,000.
12. To sanction expenditure on binding of books, journals, periodicals, registers, etc. up to ₹ 5,000.
13. To sanction expenditure towards purchase of dictionaries, reference books, etc. for office use ₹ 1,000 at a time.

Deputy Registrars

(a) Deputy Registrar—Department of Public Administration and Reforms (DPAR):

1. To sanction casual leave to the staff working under him.
2. To sanction medical reimbursement charges to persons working under him as per rules up to ₹ 2,000.
3. To sanction tea and refreshment charges for official meetings ₹ 500 at a time.
4. To sanction local purchase of stationery articles in case of exigency ₹ 500 in each case, not exceeding ₹ 2,000 per annum.
5. To sanction non-recurring contingent expenditure ₹ 500 at a time.
6. To sanction conveyance charges within the city limit to the officials on office work as per rules ₹ 500 at a time.
7. To sanction the purchase of dictionaries/manuals, etc. for office use at prevailing rates up to ₹ 500 at a time.

(b) Deputy Registrars—Other Sections:

1. To sanction casual leave to the staff working under them.
2. To sanction tea and refreshment charges on official meetings as per standard scale fixed ₹ 500 at a time.

3. To sanction local purchase of stationery articles in case of exigency ₹ 500 in each case, not exceeding ₹ 2,000 per annum.
4. To sanction the purchase of dictionaries/manuals, etc. for office use at prevailing rates up to ₹ 500 at a time.

Director, Physical Education

1. To sanction non-recurring contingent expenditure out of office imprest and local purchases of stationery articles ₹ 500 at a time.
2. To sanction repairs of furniture and other articles up to ₹ 500 at a time not exceeding ₹ 1,000 per annum.
3. To sanction casual leave to teaching and non-teaching staff of his section.
4. To sanction expenditure on repair of courts/grounds/sports equipment ₹ 1,000 at a time.

Chief Medical Officer

1. Local purchase of stationery articles, office and clinical contingencies like soap, detergent, towels, insecticides up to ₹ 500 at a time.
2. To sanction repairs of hospital and office equipment ₹ 5,000 at a time.
3. To sanction drugs, minor equipment, etc. to the university Health Centre ₹ 5,000 at a time.

Director—Printing Press

Very few universities, like the Karnatak University have their own printing press. The Director of the press at this university has the following powers for smooth functioning.

1. To sanction and purchase different kinds of papers/boards/cards/types/bindings and other printing materials immediately required for printing as per rules ₹ 5,000 at a time.
2. To sanction purchase of consumables articles like ink, gum, thread, etc. required for the press as per rules ₹ 2,000 at a time.

3. To sanction repair charges for the machinery in the press as per rules ₹ 5,000 at a time.
4. To purchase soaps and towels for press employees as per rules ₹ 500 at a time.

Principals of Constituent Colleges/Schools

Many State universities also run one or more constituent colleges and even Primary/Higher Secondary schools. Hence, delegation of powers to the principal/headmaster of the respective institutions may also be extended as detailed below:

1. To sanction local purchase of stationery articles ₹ 5,000 each case.
2. To sanction expenditure on repairs of office/lab equipment ₹ 5,000 at a time.
3. To sanction expenditure in connection with the binding of books and journals.
4. To sanction advance of T.A. for journey and tours, local conveyance charges for employees (for office work) of the concerned institution, except for themselves.
5. Purchase of soaps and towels to the office and laboratory use ₹ 5,000 per annum for Science College and ₹ 1,000 for other Colleges.
6. To countersign T.A. and other bills of employees working in the concerned institution.
7. To draw salary and allowances of the office establishment under their control including part time/honorary/visiting teachers.
8. To sanction casual/earned/half-pay leaves and all other kinds of leave to employees working under them up to two months.
9. To sanction maternity/paternity leave to their employees per rules.
10. To operate Personal deposit, Gymkhana accounts and to accept and refund all deposits as per rules and regulations prescribed by the university.

11. To dispose of waste papers, newspapers, etc. by calling local quotations.
12. To auction unserviceable articles as per university rules.
13. To sanction reimbursement of medial charges to employees of concerned institution up to ₹ 2,000.
14. To purchase pencils, broomsticks, washing powders, insecticide, etc. for the maintenance of office, laboratory, cloak room and library ₹ 1,000 at a time.
15. Purchase of Library books, renewing subscriptions to journals as per rules.
16. To select and admit students to various courses as per rules.
17. To sanction stipend to students as per rules.
18. To recommend punishment for indiscipline and misbehaviour of students. Penalizing up to a day's salary and or recommend to university for greater punishment in case of employees.
19. To sanction educational tours, annual leadership training camp-nicks and picnics, and specimen collection tours as per rules.
20. Purchase of sports and other materials as per rules.
21. Utilization of various types of funds (e.g. Gymkhana, Moot Court Funds, etc.).
22. To initiate disciplinary action against employees for gross negligence, misconduct, frauds, theft, dishonesty, habitual breach of orders, wilful damages to the institutional property, refusal to accept charge sheets, university orders or other communication issues to be served according to the rules.
23. To sanction festival advances as per rules.
24. Purchase of equipment up to ₹ 25,000.
25. To sanction expenditure on binding of books, journals, periodicals, registers, etc., up to ₹ 5,000.
26. To sanction expenditure towards purchase of dictionaries, reference books, etc. for office use ₹ 1,000 at a time.

Dean/Director-Students Welfare

1. To sanction local purchase of stationery articles for office use ₹ 5,000 per annum.
2. To sanction expenditure on repairs of the office equipment, purchase of spare parts and such other expenditure ₹ 10,000 each time.
3. To sanction casual leave to employees working under him.
4. To impose punishment to the UG/PG students for indiscipline and misbehaviour with fine up to ₹ 500.
5. To subscribe daily newspapers, weekly magazines, etc. up to ₹ 10,000 each time.
6. To sanction tea and refreshment charges on official meetings up to ₹ 500 at a time.
7. To call tenders after observing all formalities up to ₹ 20,000 at a time.

Warden of University Hostels (UG/PG)

1. To purchase stationery articles up to ₹ 5,000 at a time.
2. To incur expenditure on repairs of office/hostel furniture/material, etc., up to ₹ 10,000 per annum.
3. To sanction casual leave to the staff working under him/her.
4. To operate personal deposit and refund of deposits pertaining to students of their hostels.
5. To admit students to the hostel, on the recommendation of the Dean-Students Welfare (DSW)/Chairman of the PG Departments/Principals of Constituents Colleges.
6. To impose punishment to the hostel students for indiscipline and misbehaviour/misconduct, etc. with the concurrence of the DSW.
7. To subscribe daily newspapers/weekly/monthly, etc. magazines to the hostel up to ₹ 500 each time.
8. To incur expenditure towards tea and refreshment charges on official meetings/functions up to ₹ 500 at a time.

Appendix–2

Alumni Association: Some Ideas

The following points provide illustrative ideas pertaining to the operation of Alumni Associations (AA) in educational institutions.

1. The VC and his representative can play the roles of a patron and a coordinator respectively, to facilitate smooth conduct of activities of the AA.
2. The President and Secretary have to be from out of the membership of AA. Some retired professors or senior level officials who have passion to undertake such works by devoting their time and are also computer savvy may be elected for various positions of the AA.
3. The office bearers may be chosen from different backgrounds like accounting, culture, music, sports, academic, legal, etc.
4. Often, the PG Departments insist on enrolling the members on payment of fixed fees. It is better to do away with this. Enrol all those who are interested in becoming members of the AA soon after their taking admission to a course. Those who are unable to pay the prescribed fee need not be discouraged from becoming members of the association. Such members may be allowed to pay the prescribed fee later when they begin earning. In any case, admission fee should be nominal. However, such members who have not paid fee may be denied the voting rights and election to office bearers.
5. Details of the members should contain name, year of passing, permanent and temporary addresses, telephone numbers and email id, and current jobs held etc.
6. The association should have a website and mechanism to collect fee and donations, endowment funds, online and depiction of its activities performed in the previous years.
7. The annual accounts, utilization details, remarks of the auditors should be displayed on the website annually.

8. The host institution should provide the needed office space and basic infrastructure to the registered AA free as long as the association is active and not dormant.
9. The institution should encourage activities of the association by providing lecture halls, guest house facilities, etc. for conducting the meetings and other activities.
10. The AA and the institution must meet at least once in six months to evolve appropriate strategies, and involve the office bearers in the activities of the institution, promotion of sports, culture, infrastructure development, and institution of scholarships through meaningful deliberations.
11. The AA may honour the donors and achievers in their annual functions followed by a get together lunch/dinner.
12. In addition to the suggestions made above, the AA may take up many other activities as decided in its office bearers meeting.

(*Source*: A.B. Shanbhag, 2019b)

Appendix–3

User-Friendly Guidelines for Operation of Research Grants

(Appendix to Chapter 5)

The following sections outline the "User-Friendly Guidelines for Operation of Research and Development Grants" formulated and adopted by Karnatak University, Dharwad (vide Syndicate resolution No. 44 of 10 February 2007). Varsities desirous of providing such guidelines to their researchers may suitably revise the various provisions as per the current needs.

(A) Administrative Approval/Sanction

1. The Coordinator/Principal Investigator (PI) shall obtain a onetime formal administrative sanction, for the Head-wise expenditure of the grants (as awarded by the funding agency) for the entire duration of the project, i.e., from the date of implementation to the termination of the project, from the Vice-Chancellor.
2. The Coordinator/PI are permitted to draw advances directly from the Finance Officer (FO), without seeking administrative sanction from the Registrar using the Format-I appended to the guidelines. The Finance Officer is authorized to release the advances to the Coordinator/PI as are when requested. Further, the advance taken should be settled by the submitting bills directly to the FO.

(B) Purchase of Equipment and Consumables/Minor Civil Works

1. The Coordinator/PI may spend up to ₹ 10,000 (Rupees Ten Thousand only) at a time on any item without calling for comparative quotations. This includes minor civil works related to renovation/alteration/electric works/civil works pertaining to laboratory/animal house, directly or through Resident Engineer.
2. For purchase of individual item(s) costing above ₹ 10,000 and less than ₹ 50,000 comparative quotations shall be called from at least 8-10 firms supplying the needed

items. There should be a minimum of three quotations while finalizing the purchase order. This will not apply for purchases that are covered under the Rate Contract. Approval of the Purchase Committee is not required for items costing less than ₹ 50,000.

(C) For Purchase of Items Costing more than ₹ 50,000

A 'Purchase Committee' consisting of the Coordinator/PI, Deputy Coordinator/Co-investigator, if any, Chairman of the Department (COD), FO, and Development Officer should be constituted and the purchase orders shall be approved by the Committee. The Coordinator/PI will convene the meeting.

1. For purchase of items costing more than ₹ 1 Lakh, the provisions of the Transparency in Public Procurement (TPP) Act, 2001 should be followed. The details of the same may be obtained from the FO.
2. Items whose prices are approved by the respective State or Central Governments (GOI) can be directly purchased without calling for quotations.
3. For purchase of items directly from the manufacturers e.g. Sigma/Aldrich/Merck/items under rate contract, sole suppliers or distributors, of Indian/foreign materials in India, and from standard company show rooms, it is not necessary to obtain comparative quotations. The single quotation obtained from any of the above suppliers may be used to place order with the approval from the Vice-Chancellor.

The equipment and furniture procured under research grants shall be first entered into Stock Register Book of the Department and then issued to the concerned Investigator. In addition, the investigator shall maintain a separate stock book of equipment/furniture for the purpose of operation of the individual grants. The consumables need not be entered into the Stock Register of the Department. The PI shall also maintain a logbook documenting the use of the equipment.

After retirement/leaving the Department, the PI shall return all the equipment/furniture to the COD who will in turn distribute the same among the faculty members of the department in consultation with the Departmental Council. All the equipment shall remain in the department to which the PI belongs, irrespective of the Department to which a Co-PI may belong.

(D) Purchase of Books

The books may be purchased both by calling for quotations or directly from the suppliers/dealers without calling for quotations with at least 15% discount except in case of publications of Government/Scientific organizations. In case of foreign books, the bills should accompany the price proof and GOC conversion rate applicable at the time of supply.

(E) Fieldwork

In projects where fieldwork is a component, the Coordinator/PI is encouraged to take up fieldworks as far as possible on holidays and weekends. Where fieldworks are carried out for less than five days, the Coordinator/PI may undertake the fieldwork with prior approval of the concerned COD. The teachers working in the coordinated projects may also undertake field trips, for a period not exceeding five days, with prior approval of the Coordinator and the concerned COD, so as to ensure that routine works of the department are not hampered. For fieldwork exceeding more than five days prior approval of the Registrar is essential.

(F) Library Reference Work/Laboratory outside the University/ Attending Conferences/Workshops/Seminars

1. The Coordinator/PI and all the personnel working under the sanctioned project are permitted to visit institutions for the above purposes with prior consent of the concerned COD without affecting the examination, University and Department works/functions etc. The registration for Seminar/Symposium/Conference/Workshop may be claimed out of the project grant.

2. Attendance Certificates: Ordinarily the faculty members are expected to submit attendance certificates in respect of travels undertaken by them for attending meetings, reference works, research works, and conferences/symposia. In exceptional/genuine cases may be exempted by the Vice-Chancellor. For fieldworks no attendance certificate is expected. However, the concerned faculty member shall certify himself/herself regarding the work undertaken.
3. TA/DA to project Personnel: TA/DA to project personnel is admissible as per University rules. The PI/Coordinator is authorized to sanction TA/DA to research personnel (e.g. JRF, SRF, project assistance, postdoctoral fellows, research associates, co-investigators, etc.) participating in the project.

(G) Hiring Vehicles

The Coordinator/PI may hire taxi whenever needed for conduct of fieldwork or other project related works. In case of car, the current rate admissible by the University (per km) and payment for minimum of 300 km per day is allowed. In cases involving fieldworks in interior areas like forests, hills, etc., hiring of vehicles AC/non-AC jeep/tempo/car, etc. is permitted as per the existing market rates, but after obtaining the formal approval from the Vice-Chancellor. In case of short distance fieldworks (less than 100 km each way) the investigators may also use own cars and claim ₹ 5.50 per km.

(H) Photocopying and Typing Charges

In order to obtain quality service in photocopying and typing works, the prevailing market rates as certified by the Coordinator/PI are allowed.

(I) Appointment of Secretarial Assistant/Lab-cum-Field Attendant

In case there is a provision to appoint secretarial assistant/Lab-cum-field attendant they may be paid out of the working expenses/contingency/overhead charges subject to the provisions of the funding agency. The said personnel may be appointed after following the usual procedures of the University. In case of part time secretarial assistants (those who can operate computer, process papers for placing orders, passing the bills, maintaining the files and stock books, etc.) a payment of ₹ 600-800 may be paid, depending upon the experience. In case of full time Secretarial Assistant/Lab-cum-Field Attendant, etc., the daily allowance shall be paid as prescribed by the University from time to time. Prior approval of the Registrar should be obtained for such appointments as well as payments.

(J) Overhead Charges

Some R&D agencies provide overhead grants. These funds may be utilized for maintenance of equipment and for furtherance of the project works. The funds may be used to procure the equipment and accessories, laboratory tables/chairs and so on.

(K) Settlement of Bills and Advances

1. All bills/vouchers/invoices/receipts will be certified by Coordinator/PI. The concerned COD need not countersign each individual bill. However, all bills should be forwarded through the COD.
2. All bills/vouchers/invoices/receipts submitted to the Finance Officer should be settled within 4-6 weeks and the PI/Coordinator be intimated regarding the same. Finance Officer need not seek approval of Registrar/ Vice-Chancellor for passing the bills (each time), once administrative sanction is accorded by the Registrar/ Vice-Chancellor at the beginning of the commencement of the project.
3. After submission of bills/vouchers/invoices/receipts and settlement of advance the Finance Officer will inform the same to the concerned Coordinator/PI.
4. The accounts shall be audited by Government Auditor or a Chartered Accountant (if permitted by the funding agency).